I0098945

# THE WONDERS OF BIBLE CHRONOLOGY

by
Philip Mauro
Author of *The Hope of Israel* and
*The Seventy Weeks and the Great Tribulation*

---

"I have considered the days of old,
the years of ancient times" (Psa. 77:5).

---

www.solafidepublishers.com

The Wonders of Bible Chronology
by Philip Mauro

Originally Published in 1933
by The Perry Studio
Washington, D. C.


Sola Fide Publishers
Post Office Box 2027
Toccoa, Georgia 30577
www.solafidepublishers.com

Cover and Interior Design by
Magnolia Graphic Design
www.magnoliagraphicdesign.com

ISBN-13: 978-0692361764
ISBN-10: 0692361766

# CONTENTS

# PREFACE TO THE REVISED EDITION

The first edition of this work appeared in 1922 and other editions followed. It was published under the title, *The Chronology of the Bible*, which might suggest that the volume consisted largely of tables of dates and other statistical matter. Such, however, is not the case. The volume does indeed contain tables which exhibit "the chronology of the Bible," by which is meant that specific chronology which is found *in the Bible itself.* For it is not the least of the wonders of the Sacred Volume that, embedded in the text thereof, is a continuous line of dated episodes, which begins with the creation of Adam and reaches across forty centuries of time even to the resurrection of Jesus Christ and the coming of the Holy Spirit. Such being the case, it is a matter of deep interest to all readers, and of surpassing value to all students of the Holy Scriptures, to have at hand, in tabulated form, the chronological data constituting that unique line. Nevertheless, this volume has a much larger object, and the author's reason for publishing this new edition under the title *The Wonders of Bible Chronology* is to suggest thereby that larger object. For the chronology of the Bible, in contrast with all other chronologies, has certain distinctive and unique features which are of a nature so remarkable as to be worthily called "wonderful."

The very existence of such a chronological and genealogical line is itself a wonder of high import; for it is absolutely unique. There is not another such line, either in the Bible itself or in the extant literature of any nation. But it is a still greater marvel that, in tracing the course of that dated line, one is brought into contact with historical events and matters of truth and doctrine of superlative value to mankind.

This marvelous chronology has a basis of its own, a plan of its own and a purpose of its own. Its *basis* is the Bible itself; its *plan* is the genealogical or life line that stretches from the first Adam to the last Adam, from the beginning of the old creation to that of the new; and its *purpose* is to bring those who follow its progress to revelations of vital truth pertaining to God's mighty work of Redemption, and to spiritual and practical lessons of superlative value.

For reasons concerning which it were idle to speculate, God has been pleased to reveal His Mind and Purpose for humanity in connection with a line of events arranged in chronological relations, each with its immediate predecessor and successor, in such manner as to form a connected chain *four thousand years long*. This is what chiefly invests the chronology of the Bible with its exceptional interest and value. But apart from this, it is the author's purpose to supply, in a convenient form adapted to the use of all students and readers, *a complete tabulation of the dated events of the Bible.* There is, so far as the author is aware, nothing of the sort now available. Works on chronology are usually so bulky, costly and burdened with technical discussions, as to be of little or no interest or value to the majority of Bible-readers.

The text of this edition has been carefully revised and, we believe, greatly improved. The tables, however, are the same as in previous editions.

All dates are given both in terms of An. Hom. (Creation of Man) and B.C. (Before Christ).

Washington, D.C., November, 1933.

# CHAPTER ONE

## Outline of the Chronology Embodied in the Bible

The chronology of the Bible is a subject of great importance as well as of deep interest; yet, because of the difficulties connected with it, the study thereof is neglected by nearly all Bible readers. Only the few who have a special aptitude for figures, and a special interest in Bible dates and epochs, give any attention to it. We are confident, however, that the difficulties to which we have alluded can be greatly diminished, and the subject made comparatively plain and easy. Indeed we have been prompted to the writing of these pages by the conviction that, if the chronology, which extends from the beginning to the end of the Old Testament Scriptures, and which forms a very striking feature thereof, could be set forth in such manner as to be readily understood by ordinary readers, it would be studied not only with profit but with enjoyment also by many who now imagine it to be beyond their capacity. Moreover, such an aid to an understanding of Bible chronology may be expected to stimulate the study of all parts of Scripture.

Our own interest in this subject was awakened by Dr. Martin Anstey's great work, *The Romance of Bible Chronology*, published in 1913 by Marshall Bros., London. In that work, comprising two large volumes, every chronological statement contained in the Hebrew text of the Old Testament is examined, and all the dated events are noted and tabulated. From the abundant data thus gathered, Dr. Anstey has formulated a complete chronological system, from the creation of Adam to Christ. This system is of unique character and unique value, in that *it rests on the statements of the Word of God alone.*

It is found that the Bible contains within itself, not merely a vast amount of chronological *material,* but also a *complete chronological scheme,* insomuch that it is not necessary to seek from other sources information concerning Bible events. And not only so, but just where the (always imperfect and uncertain) secular chronologies lose themselves in the impenetrable mists of the past, the chronology of Scripture is most definite, complete, and perfect in its details. In this, as in other respects, the Bible presents a marked contrast to human histories and chronicles of the past.

Dr. Anstey's work, while invaluable to those who wish to study the subject in all its details, is too bulky and costly to be available to the majority of the Lord's people. The most valuable part, however, of the information it contains, can be set forth in comparatively small compass; and this we shall attempt to do herein.

One of the most valuable and commendable features of Dr. Anstey's work is that, being based entirely upon the statements of Scripture, its results can be tested by all Bible-readers. Other chronological systems are derived, in part at least, from sources beyond the reach of ordinary readers, who, therefore, are unable to verify the various details thereof. This feature of Dr. Anstey's work will be appreciated by those who wish to "prove all things" in order that they may "hold fast that which is good."

Chronological systems are obviously worse than useless unless they are correct; and, as matters now stand, the Bible is absolutely the only source from which materials for a complete chronology can be obtained, or from which reliable information can be had as to the dates of historical events prior to the Macedonian era (331 B.C.). If, therefore, we assume the history of the human race to have lasted about six thousand years it will be seen that for more than half (nearly two-thirds in fact) of that history there are *no records whatever,* from which a chronology could be constructed, *apart from the Old Testament Scriptures.*

Furthermore, upon examining the ancient remains (fragments of histories, tablets, inscriptions on monuments, etc.) we find that, the more ancient they are, the more vague, uncertain, and meagre is the chronological information they contain. Apparently it did not enter into the minds of any of the scribes and scholarly men of those early nations to preserve connected historical records, year by year (dating from some definite era), as has been the universal practice of the modern nations. But, in the Bible, even if we regard it simply as the annals of the Hebrew race, we have a remarkable exception to the practice of all the other nations of antiquity, in respect to the manner of keeping their national records, an exception so remarkable that it would be difficult or impossible to account for it apart from the doctrine of the Divine inspiration of the Hebrew Scriptures. We are speaking of the fact that, throughout the Sacred Writings, there is the most marked attention paid to the matter of dates, intervals of time, and epochs which begin with a definite era, and to such as are marked by the birth of selected individuals in a definite line, from father to son, those individuals being, from the days of Samuel, the successive kings of Judah. It is most clearly manifest that whoever planned and decreed the contents of the Bible attached a high value to chronology *from the very beginning.* The first chapter of Genesis is a complete chronology of six days, giving the order, day by day, of the main operations whereby the earth was prepared as a habitation for man, and including the creation of man, male and female. The Creation of Man supplies the first era; and from it the extended chronology of the Bible starts. The fifth chapter of Genesis is *pure chronology,* and not only so, but it is a *perfect specimen* of chronology in its definiteness and completeness from beginning to end. Every statement connects in the most exact way with the preceding; and furthermore, a simple arithmetical check is provided whereby the accuracy of the entire tabulation is insured. The Author of this remarkable chronological table had some reason (which we think can be discerned) for taking special precautions to exclude error in making copies from the original. This table begins with the first year of Adam, and extends to the five hundredth year of Noah. It covers the entire epoch from the creation of man to the flood, 1656 years.

This complete genealogical and chronological table is truly a marvelous thing in itself, and the more so when contrasted with the historical fragments which have come down to us from the days of Moses, or even with those of a thousand years nearer to our own times. It is safe to say that, if Genesis 5 were not in the Bible, and if a tablet were exhumed, say in Assyria or Egypt, bearing the same concise statistical statements, it would be hailed as the most wonderful and valuable relic of antiquity. And not only so, but many who attach little or no importance to the statements as found in the Bible, would give full credence to *the very same statements,* if recorded by some unknown Egyptian or Babylonian sinner.

Again in Genesis 11 is a similar chronological table. This table takes the one hundredth year of Shem as its era (or starting point) and extends to the birth of Abram.

In subsequent chapters of Genesis we find the chronology from Abraham to Joseph, which the succeeding books of Moses extend to the Exodus, and to the wanderings of the Israelites in the wilderness.

In the historical books (Joshua to 2 Chronicles) is found the chronology of the nation of Israel from its entrance into the land of Canaan to its captivity in Babylon.

Finally, from the later historical books of Ezra and Nehemiah, and the prophecy of the ninth chapter of Daniel, we obtain the span of the years from the captivity to the manifestation of Jesus Christ to Israel (through the witness and baptism of John, whose coming was foretold in the last book of the Old Testament).

Thus the Old Testament Scriptures contain a complete count of the years from Adam to Christ; and this surely is not one of the least of the wonders of our wonderful Bible. Moreover, the

Author of the Bible deemed that count of years so needful to His design as a whole that, although the Old Testament comes to an end four hundred years before Christ, a prophecy was given ere it closed (that brought by Gabriel to Daniel) which contains the exact measure of time from the re-birth of the nation of Israel, by virtue of the decree of Cyrus the Great (Ezra 1:1-4), "unto the Messiah" (Dan 9:25). This prophecy, therefore, reaches forth into the then distant future, to make perfect and complete the tale of the years from the first Adam who sinned and died, unto the last Adam who died unto sin and rose again, even to the supreme event of all time, the crucifixion and resurrection of the Divine Redeemer (Dan. 9:26).

But the entire course of the 4,000-year period compassed by Bible chronology does not lie in plain view upon the surface of the Sacred Text. At several points it disappears beneath the surface thereof, so that there are seemingly several breaks in the continuity of the chronological record; as for example, the Scripture does not state the age of Noah at the birth of Shem (Gen. 5:32), nor that of Terah at the birth of Abram (Gen. 11:26). But, in the case of each of these seeming breaks, the needed information is supplied by other Scriptures, though in some cases it has been found only after diligent search and careful deductions. It will be a matter of deep interest to trace out these half-concealed links between the several epochs of Bible history. Thus in respect to its chronological data, as in respect also to other categories of truth and doctrine, some things of value are not found upon the surface, but must be diligently sought in the sub-strata of the Divine Word.

We note then, at the beginning of our study, that the Bible is absolutely the only available source of information concerning the chronology of the human race prior to the seventh century B.C., when the first vague historical records of existing nations such as Greece, Rome, China, &c., begin. In other words, if we take it that the lifetime of mankind has been something less than six thousand years (and there is no evidence at all for a longer term of human existence), then we have the remarkable fact that for about *three-fifths of the entire period* there is no chronological information whatever *except in the Bible;* whereas, on the other hand, during that same period (wherein other records are, as regards chronology, a perfect blank) *the chronology of the Bible is most definite and complete.* From this we may learn, among other things, that we have no need to look outside the Bible itself for information as to Bible chronology, and also that, if we give credence to chronological information derived from other sources, we are most likely to be misled thereby.

Furthermore we find that, whereas human histories of the great nations of the world have *no beginning at all,* but emerge gradually from a perfect fog of myths, legends and fables (often absurd and grotesque), the Bible has, from its very first word, a definite historical character, in the greatest possible contrast with all other ancient writings.

# CHAPTER TWO

## Chronology in General

We have seen that the Bible, at its very beginning, sets forth chronological information in the most definite and precise terms, and that it dates its entire scheme of chronology from the creation of the human race. In the greatest contrast with this is the fact that, in the meagre and fragmentary literary remains of ancient times, apart from the Bible, the statements respecting chronology are vague, scanty, confused, and, for practical purposes, worthless. For example, Porphyry, an opponent of Christianity, writing in the third century after Christ, quotes from an alleged history by *Sanchroniathon*, supposed to have been a contemporary of Gideon. Only a few fragments of the supposed writings of Sanchroniathon have been preserved; and those fragments are not parts of the originals but have been preserved only through the medium of quotations by other writers (as Eusebius), which, even if authentic, are valueless for purposes of chronology.

Fragments also remain of the writing of *Berosus* of Babylon (fourth century B. C.), and of *Manetho*, a learned Egyptian priest (third century B. C.). But the original writings have been lost; the portions quoted by later writers are, to say the least, of doubtful value; and the information they contain, even were it trustworthy, is very incomplete. This is in the greatest possible contrast with the writings of Moses, whereof we have the original books complete. These antedate Berosus and Manetho by many centuries, and the chronological statements therein are most definite and precise.

It is only when we come to Ptolemy, in the second century *after* Christ, that we find anything, *apart from the Bible*, which could serve as the basis for a system of chronology. Ptolemy (whose full name was Claudius Ptolemæus) was an Egyptian of great learning and genius. He is famous as the author of the Ptolemaic System of Astronomy, which was universally accepted by men of science until supplanted by the System of Copernicus, devised in the 16th century, and improved later on by Sir Isaac Newton.

Ptolemy has left on record a "Canon" or *list of Persian Kings* from Cyrus to Alexander the Great of Macedon. Upon this "canon" all modern chronologists have built their systems, and this for the simple reason that there is nothing else, apart from the Bible, for them to build on. But Ptolemy is not a contemporary historian, for he lived about *seven hundred years* after the reign of Cyrus; nor does he refer to any contemporary historical records as authority for his statements. All we have is a bare list of the names of supposed Persian kings, with the number of the years each is supposed to have lived.

Not only does Ptolemy lack corroboration in respect to his chronological statements, but he is contradicted by the writings of Josephus, the Jewish historian, who lived a *century earlier* than Ptolemy; and also by the Persian traditions preserved by Fidusi; and by the Jewish national traditions preserved in the *Sedar Olam*. Josephus was a very learned man. He lived much closer than Ptolemy, both to the Persian era, and to the Persian territory; and he would most likely have known of any authentic records of that era and region, *if any existed in that day*.

But, most important of all, the canon of Ptolemy is in conflict with the chronology of the Old Testament, in the light of which it appears that Ptolemy makes the duration of the Persian Empire more than eighty years too long. This is positive and decisive proof of the erroneous and hence untrustworthy character of the canon of Ptolemy.

It is important to notice that, if the writings of Ptolemy had not existed, there would be no profane chronology worthy of any consideration at all prior to Alexander the Great. Says Dr. Anstey:

> nor would it have been possible to have ascertained from the writings of the Greeks, or from any other source, *except from Scripture itself*, the true connection between sacred chronology and profane, in any one instance before the dissolution of the Persian Empire in the first year of Alexander the Great. Ptolemy had no means of determining the chronology of this period, so he made the best use of the materials he had, and contrived to make a chronology.... It is contradicted (1) by the national traditions of Persia, (2) by the national traditions of the Jews, (3) by the testimony of Josephus, (4) and by conflicting evidence of well-authenticated events, which makes the accepted chronology impossible. But the human mind cannot rest in a state of perpetual doubt. There was this one system elaborated by Ptolemy. There was *no other except that given in the prophecies of Daniel*. Hence the Ptolemaic chronology remains to this day. There is one, and only one alternative. We have to choose between the Heathen Astronomer and the Hebrew Prophet (pp. 19, 20).

We shall have occasion to refer again to this important branch of our subject. At present our purpose is merely to show how favourably, from every point of view, the Bible compares with all other sources as the basis for a chronology of the centuries before Christ. Indeed, it is so far superior to all other sources combined, that there is no comparison between it and them. The Bible is, as we have seen, the only *contemporary* historical writing, and the only one that even purports to give definite and precise chronological information. For the believer, moreover, it has a far higher claim to implicit confidence, in that it is the inspired Word of God, who has been pleased to give a complete count of the years from the time the first Adam was created, to the time the last Adam was "cut off.

## The Received Chronology

The chronological knowledge of most Bible readers does not extend beyond the dates which appear at the top of the marginal columns of some of the more expensive editions of the Bible. How those dates were determined they do not know; and it is beyond their power to verify them. As there given they do not begin at the beginning and count forward in the ordinary way, but they begin at the Christian era and *count backward*, so many years before Christ ("B.C."). This is very confusing. The writer has never to this day been able to adjust his mind to the unnatural operation of counting time backward. But the most serious objection to the method lies in this: The first three thousand years and more of Bible history can be reckoned with accuracy, because the Scripture gives full and clear information as to the count of years; and inasmuch as there are no other sources of information whatever, there is, and can be, no conflict of "authorities." As to that long period, one *must* either accept the chronological information given in the Bible, or do without; for there is none other. If, therefore, the chronological reckoning in our Bibles began at the beginning, and proceeded forwardly, i.e. from past to future, we should be sure at least of every date down to the days of Ezra and Nehemiah. But from their days onward to the birth of Christ, confusion and uncertainty exist as a consequence of *the acceptance of the unreliable chronology of Ptolemy in preference to that of Daniel;* which unhappy choice of our chronologers not only invalidates the chronology of the last 500 years of the Old Testament era, but it also, through the necessary consequence of the strange device of *counting the years of that era backward*, invalidates the *entire chronological scheme*, making all the dates erroneous.

## The Chronological Work of Bishop Ussher

The received chronology owes its existence very largely, if not mainly, to the great labours of James Ussher, Archbishop of Armagh, who was born in Dublin, A.D. 1581. He was a man of conspicuous ability, and a profound scholar. "He constructed," says Anstey, "a system of chronology which has held its own to this day." His system, however, has been revised and amended by others, as by Bishop Lloyd, who published in 1701 an edition of the Bible, which was the first Bible having marginal dates.

No improvement over Lloyd's chronology appears to have been made until about 1850, when the subject was taken up by Henry Fynes Clinton, who, Anstey says, "is perhaps the ablest, the soundest, and the most complete and satisfactory of all our modern chronologers." But he, like his predecessors, adopts the figures of the canon of Ptolemy, instead of those of the Book of Daniel.

## Bible Chronology Compared With That Of Other Ancient Literature

Chronology is, as we have seen, a prominent feature of the Book of Genesis, especially of its early chapters, concerning which Anstey says:

> The more carefully those chapters are studied, and the more carefully they are compared with the mythical and legendary accounts of the origins of the race in other literatures, the more evident will be the striking contrast between them. One cannot read those chapters aright without being struck with the unique grandeur and sublimity of their language, and filled with wonder and amazement at the marvel and glory of their message and content.
>
> No one can place them side by side with the mythical accounts of other religions without being struck with the incomparable distinction, which lifts them out of the class and category of all other writings, and proclaims them as being of *another origin*, and of *another kind*. And the one palpable difference between those chapters and all other forms of religious literature is the fact of their *objective historical character*. The religions of Greece and Rome, of Egypt and Persia, of India and the East, did not even *postulate* a historical basis. The mythical period of the Greeks, though similar in form, was distinct in kind from the

historic. The objective reality of the scenes and events described as belonging to each period was *not even conceived of as belonging to the same order*, or as being of the same kind. It is quite otherwise with the religion of the Old Testament. *There the doctrine is bound up with the facts;* and, moreover, it is so dependent upon them that without them it is null and void. If there is no first Adam there is no second Adam. The facts are the necessary substratum of the truths or doctrines of the Old Testament, precisely as those truths or doctrines are the necessary substratum of *the duties* that arise out of them. The chronology of the Old Testament is in strongest contrast with that of all other nations. From the creation of Adam to the death of Joseph, the chronology is defined with the utmost precision; and it is only towards the end of the narrative of the Old Testament that doubts, difficulties and uncertainties arise. With all other chronologies the case is exactly the reverse. They have *no beginning at all.* They emerge from the unknown; and their earliest dates are the haziest and most uncertain, instead of being the clearest and most sure. If the trustworthiness of testimony and the canons of credibility are accepted in this case, the early chapters of Genesis will answer every legitimate test that can be applied to the determination of their genuine historical character.

## Bible Chronology is Intimately Associated With One Definite Subject

It is a fact of great significance that the count of years, so carefully preserved in the Bible, is bound up closely with *one definite subject*, namely, with the line of descent along which the promised Redeemer was to come. The details of this peculiarity of Bible chronology, which we propose to discuss later on, are worthy of our most careful attention; for it invests the subject with special interest. It is as if the Author of the Holy Scriptures would have us take notice of the fact that, in the long process of the unfolding of years and centuries and eras of time, there is *only one line* of succession of persons and events which is of importance in His eyes, and that is the line which was to lead to the coming into the world of the Divine Redeemer. Let it be realized that, starting with Adam, and following the ever widening circles, from generation to generation, of his rapidly multiplying offspring, there were countless *millions of directions* which any selected chronological and genealogical line might have taken. It is, therefore, to be reckoned among the clearest evidences of Divine superintendence in the writing of the Scriptures that the *one line*, to which alone dates are unfailingly attached, is that which led finally "unto the Messiah, the Prince" (Dan. 9:25).

It is well worth while to dwell further upon this immensely significant fact, because of the proof it affords of the inspiration of the Bible. Let it be observed then that the chronological table of Genesis 5 goes no further than the flood; and that the table of Genesis 11 stops abruptly at Abraham; and that neither in Genesis, nor in any Book of Moses, nor indeed in any of the Old Testament, is there any indication of God's reason for counting the years *along this particular line only;* nor was any indication given that the line of dated events was to be continued any further; nor was there any indication as to where that line was to lead. The purpose of God in all this comes not into view *until the Bible is completed by the addition of the New Testament Scriptures*, in the light of which (particularly of the genealogical tables of Matthew 1 and Luke 3) that purpose may be clearly seen. Here then is proof of the most convincing sort that He who alone sees the end from the beginning is the Author of the Books of Moses, and of all the later Books of the Old Testament, through which runs this marvelous chronological line. For the Old Testament concerns itself, from beginning to end, with but *one subject*, namely, the ordering of the historical and other events which were to lead to the coming of the Redeemer. All other matters of an historical nature which are found recorded in it are seen to be in some way connected with the main subject. *That* is never lost sight of. And it is a most impressive fact that, although the inspired history of the Jewish people came to an end four hundred years before the birth of Christ, yet God saw to it that, ere the last of the inspired writers laid down his pen, a chronological line had been thrown out into the future, by means of "the sure word of prophecy," whereby to span that wide chasm of four centuries, and to reach "unto the Messiah." Moreover, the last sentences of the Old Testament leave its readers looking forward to one of whom Jehovah said:

> Behold, I will send My messenger before My face, and he shall prepare My way before Me. Behold, I will send you Elijah the prophet before the coming of the great and dreadful day of the LORD; and he shall turn the heart of the fathers to the children, and the heart of the children to their fathers, lest I come and smite the earth with a curse (Mal. 3:1; Mal. 4:5-6).

Strong as is the proof set forth above that the chronology of the Bible had from its very beginning a special purpose known only to its Author, that proof is made even stronger by the fact that, when other lines of descent are given, there is *no chronology* connected with them. Thus, the very first table of descent is that of Adam's eldest son Cain (Gen. 4:17-24). It has *no dates*. Whereas, in the table of Seth's line, in the very next chapter, the years are given with such regularity, and with such precautions against error, as to show that the chronology was the important thing in the mind of the Author. So, likewise, though the descendants of Japheth and of Ham are given in Genesis 10 (and given before those of Shem), yet there is not so much as one chronological fact set forth in connection with their names. When, however, in the very next chapter, the chosen line which leads eventually to Christ is taken up again (the line of Shem), we read: "These are the generations of Shem: Shem was *an hundred years old*, and begat Arphaxad *two years after the flood;* And Shem lived after he begat Arphaxad *five hundred years*, and begat sons and daughters. And Arphaxad lived *five and thirty years*, and begat Salah; and Arphaxad lived after he begat Salah *four hundred and three years*"; and so on to Abraham, without a single omission of the chronological data, pertinent to the Divine purpose, in the connected count of years.

Even when we come to the genealogy of such important personages as Moses and Aaron (Ex. 6:16-26) there is *no chro-*

*nology*, that is to say, the father's age at the birth of that particular son through whom the line was to be continued is not stated. Moses was in some way given to know that the chronology of his own line (though personal pride would have prompted him to exalt it) was of no importance in the records he was writing.

Thus we arrive at the remarkable fact that, for the first two thousand years of the history of the human race, that is to say, from Adam to Abraham, there exists a record of an unbroken line of descent, and of *one only*, in which line the chronology is accurately preserved and safeguarded from error, by the simple expedient of giving the father's age, in each generation, when *that particular son* was born, through whom the line was to be continued, *the father's age at the birth of others of his sons being never given*. This striking peculiarity is the more remarkable when it is further noted that, so far as appears, it was *not the oldest son* that was chosen in any instance. For Seth was not the oldest son of Adam, nor Shem of Noah, nor Abram of Terah, nor Isaac of Abraham, nor Jacob of Isaac, nor Judah of Jacob, nor David of Jesse. As to the others named in the line of descent of Christ, it is not stated whether they were, or were not, the oldest of their respective generations. Evidently, however, primogeniture did not enter into the matter at all. This is very remarkable, particularly in view of the importance given by the Hebrews to the firstborn (Gen. 49:3).

During the period of the kings of Israel and Judah the line from father to son passed through the successive kings of Judah, from David to Jehoiachin. During this period the chronology is preserved by the given length of the reigns of the successive kings.

## A Connecting Link With Secular Chronology

In Jer. 25:1 is found a statement which constitutes a perfect connecting link between sacred and profane chronology. This is the statement: "The *fourth* year of Jehoiakim, which was the *first* year of Nebuchadnezzar." At this point of time God was preparing to bring in the era of Gentile dominion, "the times of the Gentiles"; for Nebuchadnezzar was *the first* of the God-appointed rulers of the world, "the powers that be," which are "ordained of God," and who are to exercise dominion until "the days of the voice of the seventh angel, when he shall begin to sound his trumpet," at which time "the kingdoms of this world shall become the kingdoms of our Lord, and of His Christ" (Rev. 10:7; Rev. 11:15). It is very significant therefore, that, when the throne of David, as an earthly thing, was about to be cast down to the ground (Ps. 89:39), and the sceptre of earthly dominion was about to pass to the Gentiles, God caused the chronology of the holy people to be connected by an "infallible link" with *the first year of the first Gentile ruler.*

Concerning this remarkable fact Anstey says:

> The *one infallible connecting link* between sacred and profane chronology is given in Jer. 25:1: "The fourth year of Jehoiakim, which was the first year of Nebuchadnezzar." If the events of history had been numbered forward from this point to the birth of Christ, or back from Christ to it, we should have had a perfectly complete and satisfactory chronology.

We see then that the Bible is pre-eminently a book of chronology; but its chronology is of a very exceptional sort. For chronology in general it shows no regard whatever; but for *one particular line* it manifests the utmost solicitude. That single chronological line delineates the central theme of the entire Scripture. All the recorded events of the whole Bible cluster around it; for the sacred records have to do *only* with persons and incidents which are more or less closely associated with that line. In view of all this, and especially of the supremely important fact that the line referred to *leads to Christ*, and *stops there*, the study of Bible chronology should be of the deepest interest to all His people.

# CHAPTER THREE

## The Patriarchs Before the Flood

Having given, in the foregoing pages, a general outline of the chronology found in the Bible, and having indicated the most prominent features thereof, we shall now look more closely into the details of the subject.

The chronology of the Bible does not begin with the creation of the world, but with the creation of *Man.* This should be carefully noted. Concerning the date of the creation of the visible universe the Scripture is silent. All the information given us as to that interesting matter is what is contained in the first verse of the Bible, namely, *"In the beginning* God created the heaven and the earth." There is, therefore, no warrant at all for the term *Anno Mundi* (year of the world). Anstey very properly uses the term An. Hom. *(Anno Hominis,* year of man).

We do not enter into the discussion of the disputed question whether or not long ages of time (as the theories of geologists require) intervened between the first verse of Genesis and the third. On the one hand the Hebrew word rendered "was," in Gen. 1:2 ("And the earth *was* waste and void"), undoubtedly has the force and meaning of "became"; so that there is ample room in that verse for the longest geological ages that have ever been conjectured. On the other hand, we do not question the power of God to produce the raw materials of the heaven and the earth in a moment, and to prepare the earth for the abode of mankind in six days of twenty-four hours each. But we leave that question untouched herein, because our subject begins, not with the first year of the world, but with the first year of Adam, and it has to do with *facts,* affording no room for conjectures.

As to the time of the year when the first man was made a living soul, and was placed in the garden of Eden, the indications point to the Autumnal Equinox. For the Hebrew year began at that season, though it was changed by the express command of God at the Exodus so as to begin at the Vernal Equinox (Ex. 12:2). We know that the first plants did not develop from seeds; for it is written that the Lord God made "every plant of the field *before it was in the earth,* and every herb of the field *before it grew"* (Gen. 2:4-5). Thus the first plants were full-grown and mature. They did not grow up from seeds or shoots, any more than the first man and woman grew up from a boy and a girl. From this we may gather, therefore, that an adult man was placed in a garden filled with mature, fruit-bearing trees and plants, at that season of the year (late summer or early autumn) when the harvest of grains and fruits is ripe.

The fifth chapter of Genesis is in the form of a family register, kept with the most painstaking care, yet singularly unconcerned about the children save *one only in each generation,* the selection being governed by a purpose which is not disclosed. The chapter has a descriptive title: "The Book of the Generations of Adam." It contains the names of ten men, one in each generation from Adam to Noah, inclusive. The same form is used throughout, thus: "Adam lived an hundred and thirty years, and begat a son, ...and called his name Seth; and the days of Adam, after he had begotten Seth, were eight hundred years; and he begat sons and daughters. And all the days that Adam lived were nine hundred and thirty years; and he died." By thus dividing each patriarch's life into two periods (marked by the birth of that particular son through whom the genealogical line was to be continued), by stating the number of years contained in each period, and by giving finally the total of the two periods, a means is provided whereby any error, such as might be made by a copyist, for example, in any of the figures in the table, would be instantly detected.

This is the table:

Table I

| | *An. Hom.* | *B.C.* |
|---|---|---|
| Adam created | 0 | 4046 |
| Adam's age at birth of Seth | 130 | 3916 |
| Add Seth's age at birth of Enos (105) | 235 | 3811 |
| Add Enos' age at birth of Cainan (90) | 325 | 3721 |
| Add Cainan's age at birth of Mahalaleel (70) | 395 | 3651 |
| Add Mahalaleel's age at birth of Jared (65) | 460 | 3586 |
| Add Jared's age at birth of Anoch (162) | 622 | 3424 |
| Add Enoch's age at birth of Methuselah (65) | 687 | 3359 |
| Add Methuselah's age at birth of Lamech (187) | 874 | 3172 |
| Add Lamech's age at birth of Noah (182) | 1056 | 2990 |
| Add Noah's age at the time of the flood (600) | 1656 | 2390 |

Thus, if the figures given in the Hebrew text of the Old Testament are accepted as correct, there is no possibility of arriving at any other conclusion than that the period of time from the creation of Adam to the flood (whereby his entire posterity then living, with the exception of the family of Noah, was wiped out) is exactly 1656 years. As to this there is perfect agreement among all chronologers who accept as correct the Hebrew text of the Old Testament.

## "That is Not First Which is Spiritual"

It is well worth while to notice at this point a striking peculiarity of the selection made by God of the persons and genealogies that were to figure in the Old Testament. The Book of Genesis is, among other marked characteristics, a book of *contrasts.* In reading it we find ourselves contemplating, from time to time, two contrasted individuals, or lines of descent, or sets of incidents. Thus, we have at the outset two sons of Adam, Cain and Abel; then two lines of descent from Adam, that of Cain and that of Seth; then the contrast between Abraham and Lot; then that between Ishmael and Isaac; then that between Esau and Jacob; then that between Reuben and Joseph (to whom was allotted the birthright); and finally that between Manasseh and Ephraim.

What impresses the attentive reader in all this duplex character of the Genesis narrative is that, in *every instance,* the elder (or the first to arrive on the scene and to establish himself) is rejected of God, and the younger, or later, is chosen. Thus by the Divine prerogative of election Cain is set aside and Abel is chosen. Seth, which means *substituted,* takes the place of Abel as the one chosen of God for His purposes, according to the prophetic word of Eve who, in naming him, said, "For God hath appointed [or substituted] me another seed *instead of Abel,* whom Cain slew" (Gen. 4:25). But Cain's descendants established themselves, founded arts and industries, and made a name for themselves in the world; whereas we read of no achievement by Seth and his descendants.

Similarly, as between Abraham and Lot (who was the son of Abraham's *elder brother)* we find Lot making a way for himself and attaining prominence in the flourishing cities of the plain, while Abraham remains a childless tent-dweller, a stranger and pilgrim on earth.

In like manner we see Ishmael multiplying and prospering, his twelve sons having their "towns" and "castles" and "nations," and waxing very great (Gen. 25:12-18); while Isaac lives a quiet, pastoral life, occupied mainly in digging again the wells his father Abraham had digged, which the Philistines had stopped by filling them with earth (Gen. 26:15-18).

Reading further, we find a like contrast between Esau and Jacob. Esau is very progressive and becomes prominent in the land, while Jacob is yet serving as an hireling and *waiting.* We read of the many "dukes" (or princes) descended from Esau (Gen. 36:9-43); and it is expressly stated that "these are they that reigned in the land of Edom, before there reigned any king over the children of Israel" (v. 31).

In all these cases we observe that the history and "generations" of the rejected elder are given before those of the younger, whom God chose. For the generations of Cain precede those of

Seth; the generations of Japheth (the rejected elder brother) precede those of Shem, whose line was chosen; the generations of Ishmael precede the generations of Isaac; and the generations of Esau precede the generations of Jacob.

In all this it is easy to recognize the foreshadowing of the great Bible truth concerning the failure and rejection of the first man, who is of the earth, earthy (1 Cor. 15:45-47), and the correlative and complementary truth of the bringing in of the Second Man in his stead. For "that is not first which is spiritual, but that which is natural, and afterward that which is spiritual." These dry chronological details also put vividly before us that while the "natural" man, who comes first, is pursuing whole-heartedly his earthly career, setting his heart upon, and devoting his energies to, the acquisition of earthly place, possessions and enjoyments, the "spiritual" man, who comes afterward, has to wait, to endure trials and hardships, wherein, however, he is sustained by believing what God has spoken concerning "things not seen as yet," and is well content to confess that he is a stranger and pilgrim on the earth.

From what is written of the patriarch Jacob, we should probably not have regarded him as particularly "spiritual." But spirituality is wholly of grace, which is *given* to those who are *of faith.* Jacob *believed God* as to the value of the birthright; and the fact that he set his heart upon that which was "not seen," but of which God had spoken, constituted the difference (which is everything in God's estimation) between him and his elder brother, who "despised his birthright," and whom God therefore counted a "profane person" (Heb. 12:16).

The facts to which we have just referred serve to illustrate also the Scripture: "He *taketh away* the first that He may *establish* the second" (Heb. 10:9). For in each of the above instances, "the first" was permanently *taken away,* whereas "the second" was *established.* Thus the line of Cain was removed, while that of Seth was established; the line of "Japheth, the elder" (Gen. 10:21) was set aside, and that of Shem established; and so likewise of all the rest.

This principle comes to light in the later times also. Thus the first king of Israel, Saul, is the "natural" man. He had endowments such as natural men admire; whereas David was the "spiritual" king, the man after *God's* own heart. Hence David has to wait, amidst manifold trials and afflictions, while Saul comes "first," and is allowed to fill out his full period of forty years on the throne. But ultimately Saul's dynasty is *taken away,* while that of David is *established,* according to the word of the promise, "Thy seed will I establish forever" (Ps. 89:4).

We find the same sequence of "natural" and "spiritual" in connection with the nation composed of the natural descendants of Abraham, and which came first into existence, contrasted with the "holy nation" (1 Pet. 2:9) composed of the *spiritual* "seed" of Abraham, which came upon the scene only after the former had enjoyed a complete career in the world. Yet the first is set aside while the second is established permanently as a people for God's own possession.

Again we see the same truth illustrated by the two Covenants, of which "the first" was associated with the temporary priesthood of Aaron, whereas the second is associated with the priesthood of Jesus Christ, who is *established* as an High Priest forever (Heb. 6:20).

## The Noah-Shem Connection

It has been shown that the first series of connected events to which dates are attached extends from the creation of Adam to the flood, in the 600th year of Noah, the length of the entire period being 1656 years. The next series begins with these words: "These are the generations of Shem: Shem was an hundred years old, and begat Arphaxad, two years after the flood" (Gen. 11:10). But there is no statement of the age of Noah at the birth of Shem; for the first table ends thus: "And Noah was five hundred years old: and Noah begat Shem, Ham, and Japheth" (Gen. 5:32). There is, therefore, an apparent break between the generations of Adam and the generations of Shem.

And not only so, but there are other like breaks or interruptions in the course of the entire chronology, the continuity of the record being apparently broken at five places in all. The other four places are as follows:

1. The second table of chronology, which, like the first, contains ten generations "from Shem to Abram" ends by naming the three sons of Terah, just as the first ends by naming the three sons of Noah, *without stating the father's age at the birth of the son (in this case Abram) who was to continue the line of God's dealings.* Here again there is an apparent break in the continuity of the count of years. But the connecting link is in the Scriptures, and has been discovered and clearly identified, as we shall see.

2. The Book of Genesis ends with the death of Joseph, down to which point the chronology is clear; and the Book of Exodus begins with the birth of Moses. But the time-link between the history of Joseph and that of Moses is not given in the narrative, and must be searched for elsewhere in the Scriptures. This apparent break needs also to be mended; and this too has been accomplished.

3. Again there is a break between Joshua (and the elders who overlived him) and the period of the Judges, the chronology of which period begins with the oppression of the Israelites by Cushan-Rishathaim (Jdg. 3:8).

4. Finally, there is no direct statement of the number of years between the death of Eli (where the epoch of the Judges ends) and the beginning of the reign of Saul, with whom began the epoch of the Kings.

But the information needed to fill these five gaps, and thus to make the chronology of the Bible complete from start to finish, has been found through the studies of various chronologers; and it will be brought to the attention of our readers in these pages.

The break which immediately concerns us, that between Noah, with whom the first table ends, and Shem, with whom the second begins, is easily mended. Shem was not the eldest son of Noah. Gen. 10:21 (which is correctly rendered in the A.V.) states that Japheth was the elder. The words of Gen. 5:32 do not give us Noah's age at the birth of Shem. But from Gen. 7:6 we learn that Noah was 600 years old "when the flood of waters *was* (i.e. *came)* upon the earth"; and from Gen. 11:10 we learn that Shem was 100 years old two years after the flood, the year Arphaxad was born. From these statements it follows that *Noah was 502 years old at the birth of Shem.* For since Shem was 100 years old two years after the flood, he was 98 at the time of the flood; and at that time Noah was 600 years old (Gen. 7:6). Deducting 98 from 600 gives us 502 years as the age of Noah at the birth of Shem. Thus we have a perfect connection between the chronological table of the patriarchs before the flood, and the corresponding table of the patriarchs (Shem to Abram) after the flood.

## The Detailed Chronology of the Flood

Between these two tables the Book of Genesis gives us the detailed chronology of the flood itself. It began on the 17th day of the 2nd month of the 600th year of Noah's life (Gen. 7:11). The ark rested on the 17th day of the 7th month of the same year (Gen. 8:4), five months later. This is the month Abib or Nisan, in which the Passover was (later on) appointed to be observed on the 14th day. The Passover, as a type, was fulfilled by the sacrifice of Jesus Christ, as it is written, "Christ our Passover is sacrificed for us" (1 Cor. 5:7). The resting of the ark, as a prophetic type, was fulfilled by the resurrection of Jesus Christ (1 Pet. 3:21). Thus the type of the death of Christ occurred on the very day He was crucified (the 14th Nisan) and the type of His resurrection occurred just three days later (the 17th Nisan), that being the day the ark rested on Mt. Ararat. These striking correspondences could not be mere coincidences, nor could they possibly have been contrived by the several writers of successive portions of the Bible, seeing that those writers were separated from one another by long stretches of time. Hence the correspondences we have noted afford strong evidence of Divine superintendence over the entire Scripture. And what is of even greater importance, they tend to establish that redemption through the death and resurrection of the Divine Redeemer was in contemplation from the beginning.

The five months from the beginning of the flood to that day, during which time "the waters prevailed upon the earth," are set down as a period of "an hundred and fifty days" (Gen. 7:24) which gives 30 days to the month. Then the waters were assuaged; and "after the end of the one hundred and fifty days the waters were abated; and the ark rested on the seventh month, on the seventeenth day of the month, upon the mountains of Ararat" (Gen. 8:1-4). The process of the subsidence of the waters continued until, by the first of the tenth month, the tops of the mountains were seen (v. 5). Then, after another 40 days (which brings us to the 11th day of the 11th month), Noah sent forth a raven and a dove. The latter returned, and was sent forth again after seven days (the 18th), on which occasion she returned in the evening with an olive-leaf plucked off (v. 11). Another seven days passed, and on the 25th of the 11th month the dove was sent forth the third time, and returned not again.

On the first day of Noah's 601st year Noah removed the covering of the ark, and saw that the earth was dry (Gen. 8:13); and on the 27th day of the 2nd month the earth was dried, and God bade Noah to go forth of the ark (vv. 14-16). Thus the duration of the flood was one year and ten days.

# CHAPTER FOUR

## From the Flood to Abram

Having ascertained that Noah was 502 years old at the birth of Shem, and that Shem was 98 years old at the date of the flood, we are able to continue the count of the years from the flood to the birth of Abraham, as given in Gen. 11:10-26, as follows:

Table II

| | *An. Hom.* | *B.C.* |
|---|---|---|
| The Flood | 1656 | 2390 |
| Add two years to birth of Arphaxad | 1658 | 2388 |
| Add age of Arphaxad at birth of Salah (35) | 1693 | 2353 |
| Add age of Salah at birth of Eber (30) | 1723 | 2323 |
| Add age of Eber at birth of Peleg (34) | 1757 | 2289 |
| Add age of Peleg at brith of Reu (30). | 1787 | 2259 |
| Add age of Reu at birth of Serug (32) | 1819 | 2227 |
| Add age of Serug at birth of Nahor (30) | 1849 | 2197 |
| Add age of Nahor at birth of Terah (29) | 1878 | 2168 |

This brings us to Gen. 11:26, where we read: "And Terah lived 70 years and begat Abram, Nahor, and Haran." But this does not state the year of Terah's life in which Abram was born, which must be ascertained in order that we may connect the generations of Abraham with what went before. How is this necessary information to be supplied?

As in the parallel case of the sons of Noah, where Shem is named first, not because he is the oldest son, but because he is the one through whom God's purpose was to be accomplished, so of the sons of Terah, Abram is first mentioned, though not the oldest son.

From Gen. 11:32 we learn that Terah, Abram's father, died in Haran at the age of *205 years.* The following verse (Gen. 12:1) should be read as a continuation of this, and without the word "had," for which there is no warrant in the original. For it appears by the wording of the narrative, as well as by Stephen's words in Acts 7:4, that God gave *two distinct calls* to Abram. In response to the first call he went only so far as to Haran, where he continued to abide until the death of his father. Therefore, Gen. 11:32 and what follows should be read thus:

> And the days of Terah were two hundred and five years; and Terah died in Haran; and the LORD said unto Abram, Get thee out of thy country, and from thy kindred, and from thy father's house, unto a land that I will show thee.... So Abram departed, as the LORD had spoken unto him, and Lot went with him; and Abram was *seventy and five years old when he departed out of Haran* (Gen. 11:32-12:4).

From this it appears that Terah died at the age of 205, and that upon the death of Terah Abram departed out of Haran, being then 75 years old. If then Abram was 75 years old at the death of Terah, the latter was 130 years of age when Abram was born. This enables us to complete the table of the generations of Shem as follows:

Table II (Completed)

| | *An. Hom.* | *B.C.* |
|---|---|---|
| Terah born | 1878 | 2168 |
| Add Terah's age at birth of Abraham | 130 | 130 |
| Abram born | 2008 | 2038 |

Anstey says:

> The credit of the discovery of the age of Terah at the birth of Abram is due to Archbishop Ussher. It is one of the principal improvements of his system, and is a proof of the acuteness of his intelligence, and the keenness of his insight into the chronological bearing of statements contained in the text of Holy Scripture.

Commenting further upon this interesting point Anstey says:

> The lateness of Abram's birth in the life of his father explains how he could be only ten years older than his half-niece Sarah, or Iscah (Gen. 11:29), and therefore of an age to marry her, notwithstanding that he belonged to a generation earlier than that to which she belonged. Sarah married her father Haran's much younger brother; and similarly Milcah, Sarah's sister, married her father Haran's brother, Nahor. Abram was probably Terah's son by a second wife. If so, this would explain how Abram could say to Abimelech, "She is the daughter [granddaughter] of my father [Terah] but not of my mother."

The lateness of Abram's birth in the lifetime of his father would also explain how, at the time of the events described in Genesis 18, Abram could have a nephew (Lot) who was old enough to have daughters who were married (Gen. 19:14), and others who were of marriageable age.

It is a matter of interest to observe that the call of Abram divides the chronology of the Bible into two periods of nearly equal length. In other words, the first eleven chapters of Genesis cover a period of history almost equal in length to that covered by all the rest of the Bible.

When the Genesis narrative reaches Abraham it pauses to give a detailed account of his life. Up to this point many centuries had been covered, sometimes in a few words. But now the narrative lingers. The reason for this is very clearly seen in the light of the New Testament, where Abraham's relation to the covenants, promises, and world-wide purposes of God in Redemption, are plainly set forth, and where the particular incidents of Abraham's life, which are described in Genesis, are seen to have a special significance. Now it is of the utmost importance to observe that, at the time the account of Abraham's life was written, the significance of those incidents could have been known *only to God Himself.* Thus we learn only by the revelation given in the New Testament the deep spiritual significance of such incidents as the call of Abraham, his obedience of faith, the barrenness of Sarah, the faith Abraham had in the promise of a numerous seed, the episode of his marriage with Hagar, the "allegory" (Gal. 4) of his two wives and two sons, the miraculous birth of Isaac the child of "the promise," the offering of Isaac, and the seeking of a wife for him in Mesopotamia. Here is further evidence that the Bible is of Divine authorship. Its first Book is a history covering two thousand, three hundred and sixty-nine (2369) years, from the creation of Adam to the death of Joseph; yet this exceedingly condensed narrative pauses to relate personal incidents in the lives of Abraham, Isaac and Jacob, whereof the significance could not be known until the work of Redemption was finished, and its nature fully revealed by the Scriptures of the New Testament.

Thus the chronological features of the Bible serve in a very marked way to exhibit the fact that *the theme of the Old Testament is Redemption,* towards which the line of God's dealings was ever advancing. That purpose is connected first with *a line of individuals,* including the ten ante-diluvian patriarchs and the ten post-diluvian patriarchs (most of whom are mentioned for the sole reason that they stand in the line which leads ultimately to Christ) and including also Abraham, Isaac, and Jacob. It is connected next with *a family,* the sons of Jacob. And lastly, it is connected with *a nation* composed of the twelve tribes of Israel.

Everything connected with that line is deemed of sufficient importance in God's eyes to be dated. Other matters, mentioned solely because they come into contact with that line, are not dated, until the time arrived for God to put His rebellious people under Gentile dominion, at which time Bible chronology passes from the line of the kings of Judah to the first year of the first *Gentile* world ruler (Jer. 25:1). Thus the more carefully we consider the chronology of the Bible, the more clearly we will see in it the evidences of the design of One who both knows and also plans the end from the beginning.

As to how the chronological facts, so clearly set down by Moses, were made known to him, we are not informed. It may well have been that God imparted to him the knowledge of those facts directly, just as He imparted the instructions for building the tabernacle, and for its ordinances. Or He may have prompted those patriarchs who knew Him to preserve the necessary records.

How easily this might have been, will be apparent when due notice is taken of the facts that Adam was for 243 years the contemporary of Methuselah, that Methuselah's life overlapped that of Shem for 98 years, and that Shem was, for 150 years, the contemporary of Abraham. Thus there were but two persons between Adam and Abraham. Moreover, it is now known that the times of Abraham were times of advanced civilization. "The men of his day lived in a world which teemed with schools and libraries and books" (Anstey). It would not be strange if Abraham, "the friend of God," concerning whom He said, "Shall I hide from Abraham that thing which I do, seeing that Abraham shall surely become a great and mighty nation, and all nations of the earth shall be blessed in him?" (Gen.18:17-18) had been Divinely instructed to preserve such records as were needed for the purposes of the Scriptures. If so, those records would naturally have been preserved in the "coffin" wherein Joseph's remains were placed, which "coffin" was an ark or chest (see Gen. 50:26; Ex. 40:20; 2 Chr. 24:11, where the same word is used) concerning which Joseph took an oath of the children of Israel ere he died, and which is the subject of the very last verse of Genesis. Assuredly, whatever there were of family records, preserved (as the custom then was) with the embalmed body of Joseph, went up out of Egypt with the children of Israel, and were thus in the custody of Moses, who wrote the book of Genesis.

At this point we quote again from Dr. Anstey, who says:

> The Hebrew records of the Old Testament possess, from the very earliest times, a definite historical character, in marked contrast with those of other nations. The antiquities of the Greeks are full of poetic fictions. They wrote nothing in prose *until after the conquest of Asia by Cyrus....* They had no chronology of the times preceding the Persian Empire, except in so far as they subsequently constructed one by means of inference and conjecture.
>
> The antiquities of all other nations are likewise lost in the mist of early legend, myth, and fable. The religious systems of Greece and Rome, Egypt and India, Persia and other nations of the East did not even postulate an historical basis. The further back we trace their past history, the more obscure and uncertain it becomes.
>
> With the Hebrew records it is quite different. The history of the race begins with an epoch which is quite definite; and the record of the first 2369 years – the period covered by the Book of Genesis – is stated with such minute accuracy and precision that, for those who accept the Hebrew text, there is no possible alternative to that of Ussher, as shown in the margin of the Authorized Version. The chronological record, moreover, is accurately continued, and it may be definitely traced through the succeeding centuries. It is only when we reach the latest records of Ezra and Nehemiah that chronological difficulties become acute.
>
> The annals of the Hebrew nation are authentic narratives by *contemporary writers.* The Biblical record is the record of the redeeming activity of God. This record is *embedded in human history;* but it is a miraculous history throughout (see 1 Cor. 10:11). It is not only a history of the external events of the lives of men. In its primary significance it is *a history of God and of His activity within the realm of human history.*
>
> Hence none but men informed by the Spirit of God could write it; and only by faith in the truth of the Revelation can we ever hope to be able to understand it. The essence of Revelation is *Redemption;* and Redemption is a work of God, done, as it were, within the vail, yet manifesting itself to us in the Revelation given to us in Holy Scripture as a Divine movement in human history.

We trace the history in one unbroken line, from the creation of Adam to the crucifixion of Christ. Bible chronology is an exact science. It is not built upon hypothesis and conjecture. It rests ultimately upon evidence or testimony; but it does occasionally require the use of the method of scientific historic induction.

## The Two Lists of Patriarchs in Genesis

Upon comparison of the two lists of patriarchs, those before the flood and those after, it is seen that there is a certain similarity between them. Each is preceded by a genealogical line to which no dates are attached, and which is carried only a certain distance, and then dropped. Each list comprises ten generations (if we include Abram in the second list). Each brings us to an individual (in one case Noah, and in the other Abram) in connection with whom the working out of God's plan receives some special development.

In Noah we have one chosen of God out of all the families of the earth to bridge over the flood, and to be the beginning of a new order of things in the world. In Abram also we have one chosen of God out of all the peoples and nations of a world given over to idolatry, to be the beginning of a new order of things, and through whom, eventually, all the nations of the earth should be blessed (Gen. 12:1-3).

With Noah God established His covenant, promising the continuance of seed time and harvest, cold and heat, summer and winter, and day and night; and promising also that He would not again cut off all flesh by a flood (Gen. 8:21-22; Gen. 9:9-17). God gave the rainbow as the token of this covenant. Similarly, with Abram, God established His everlasting covenant, promises to make him the father of many nations; and He gave circumcision as the token of this covenant. All the inhabitants of the world have an interest in, and receive benefits in a measure from, both these covenants; but those who have the faith of Noah and Abraham participate in the full and eternal benefits thereof.

# CHAPTER FIVE

## The Fathers of Israel

Our previous tables have carried the sacred chronology from the creation of Adam to the birth of Abram, which was in the year 2008. We come now to the exceedingly interesting and important period of the fathers of Israel, a period that is immensely rich in instruction for the household of faith.

We have observed that the first eleven chapters of the Bible cover a great stretch of time, almost exactly equal, in fact, to that covered by the rest of the Bible. The history which God has given us of the first 2000 years of our race is composed mainly of the two elements *genealogy* and *chronology*. But now, with the calling of Abram from out of the idolatries into which the entire race had plunged, the working out of the eternal purpose of God, which He purposed in Christ Jesus our Lord, enters upon a distinctly new phase. From this point onward that purpose is to be identified with *that solitary individual,* whom God thus called and separated unto Himself. Speaking through the prophet Isaiah concerning this call of Abraham, God said: "For I called *him alone"* (Isa. 51:2). And in order that the new work which was to be done through Abraham and his seed might be manifestly all of God, that patriarch is permitted to advance to a childless old age, to an age so far advanced that both he and his wife were "as good as dead." Thus we have in Abraham, as it were, *a new beginning;* not the creation of a race of men out of the dust of the ground, but the bringing forth of a people from one who was virtually dead. This new work of God proclaims by a type or shadow the great Gospel-truth of Resurrection; that is, that God would procure a people for Himself by resurrection of the dead. From this may be clearly seen the great importance of the period upon which we are now entering.

No character of Scripture or of secular history is more important than Abraham. He is the pattern man of faith, of whom it is written that "Abraham believed God, and it was counted unto him for righteousness" (Rom. 4:3). Hence all they, whether Jews or Gentiles, who are "of faith," are counted as the spiritual seed of Abraham, so that they become the heirs of all the promises, as it is written, "Know ye, therefore, that they which are *of faith,* the same are the children of Abraham" (Gal. 3:7); and again, "And if ye be Christ's, then are ye Abraham's seed, and heirs according to *the promise"* (Gal. 3:29).

Manifestly, nothing can be of more vital concern to the perishing children of Adam than the knowledge of what is stated in the foregoing Scriptures; for the promises of "blessing" are definitely limited to "Abraham and his seed." Hence, there is salvation *only* for the children of Abraham; and this being true, it is supremely important for everyone to know that *all,* whether Jews or Gentiles, *who believe in Jesus Christ,* are the "children" of Abraham. Therefore, we quote also the following clear passage from the Word of God: "Therefore it [the promise] is of faith, that it might be by grace; to the end the promise might be sure to *all* the seed; not to that which is of the law only, but to that also which is *of the faith of* Abraham, who *is the father of us all"* (Rom. 4:16).

The quality of Abraham's faith appeared in this, that he believed in God *"who quickeneth the dead"* (Rom. 4:17). Hence saving faith is faith in the *risen Christ,* as saith the Scripture: "Now it was not written for his sake alone that it [righteousness] was imputed to him; but *for us also,* to whom it will be imputed, if we believe on him that *raised up Jesus our Lord from the dead;* who was delivered for our offences, and was raised again for our justification" (Rom. 4:23-25). And again the Scripture speaks of "the Word of faith," namely, "that if thou shalt confess with thy mouth the Lord, Jesus [i.e. Jesus as Lord] and shalt believe in thine heart that *God hath raised him from the dead,* thou shalt be saved" (Rom. 10:8-9).

In the present volume we must needs confine ourselves to brief references to the lives of the fathers, Abraham, Isaac, Jacob and Joseph, with whom the remaining chapters of Genesis are occupied; but we shall seek to notice all the events which are dated, and to give the connected chronology to the death of Joseph.

Abram was 75 years old when he left Haran and came into Canaan (Gen. 11:32; Gen. 12:4). Hence, adding 75 to the year of Abram's birth, 2008, we derive the year 2083 as the date of his entrance into the land of Canaan.

The next dated event is Abram's marriage with Hagar, at the instigation of Sarah. This was "after Abram had dwelt *ten years* in the land of Canaan" (Gen. 16:1-3). Hence this was in the year 2093. Abram and Sarah had waited ten years, and there was as yet no sign of the fulfillment of God's promise to make Abram's offspring like the stars of heaven for multitude. Still he was childless, and the possibility of offspring had become even more desperately hopeless. So we are permitted to see that even Abram's faith needed to be perfected. For he, like Adam, "hearkened to the voice of his wife." But God's time had not yet come; and this was not God's way of fulfilling His promise. The result of the expedient suggested by Sarah was "Ishmael" – the *wild ass man,* representative of that which "is not subject to the law of God, neither indeed can be" (Rom. 8:7).

Abram was 86 when Ishmael was born (Gen. 16:16), year 2094; "And when Abram was ninety years old and nine" (year 2107), God made with Abram the "everlasting covenant" (Gen. 17:1-21); at which time He appointed circumcision as the sign thereof, changed his name to Abraham, and promised him a son by Sarah, through which son the "everlasting covenant" was to be carried out.

Between this promise (that Sarah should bear a son) and the record of its fulfillment (Gen. 21:1-3) we find the account of the destruction of Sodom and Gomorrah (Genesis 19), and also that of Abraham's journey into the country of the Philistines, where Sarah was exposed to danger. Those events evidently occurred in 2107 or 2108, the latter being the year of the birth of Isaac, at which epoch the age of Abraham was 100 years (Gen. 21:5).

## Isaac and Jacob

Thus far all has been plain and easy. But we come now to events in the lives of Isaac and Jacob, the dates whereof can be ascertained only by careful computations and deductions from certain statements of Scripture, to which attention has been drawn by Ussher and later chronologers.

One important statement for this purpose is that of Ex. 12:40-41: "Now the sojourning of the children of Israel who dwelt in Egypt was *four hundred and thirty years.* And it came to pass at the end of the *four hundred and thirty years,* even *the self same day,* it came to pass, that all the hosts of the LORD went out from the land of Egypt."

This period of the "sojourning" of the people of God is reckoned from Abraham's entrance into Canaan, for then they (Abram and Sarah, the beginnings of the family) became strangers and pilgrims (Heb. 11:8-13). This is confirmed by Gal. 3:17, where the same period of 430 years is mentioned: "The covenant that was confirmed before of God in Christ, the law, which was *430 years after,* could not disannul." Here we see that the 430 years began with God's promise to Abram, made at the time he entered into Canaan at the age of 75 (Gen. 12:1-4), and ended with the giving of the law, which was the same year as the Exodus.

Thus we place the Exodus as follows:

| | *An. Hom.* | *B.C.* |
|---|---|---|
| Abram entered Canaan at the age of 75 in year . . . . . | 2083 | 1963 |
| Add 430 years, gives, as the year of the Exodus . . . . | 2513 | 1533 |

But, in addition to this period of 430 years, there is another of 400 years, which also ended at the Exodus. Thus, in Gen. 15:13 we have God's word to Abraham, "Know of a surety that *thy seed* shall be a stranger in a land that is not theirs, and shall serve them, and they shall afflict them *four hundred years.*" And again we have, in Acts 7:6, the words of Stephen, "And God spake on this wise, That his seed should sojourn in a strange land, and they should bring them into bondage and entreat them evil, *four hundred years.*"

The period of 430 years includes the sojourn of Abram and Sarah. That of 400, however, begins with the experience of Abram's *"seed."* This refers, of course, to Isaac in the first place; for in Isaac the promised "seed" was to be "called"; but the era is not that of the *birth* of Isaac, but that when he was acknowledged the "seed" and "heir" by the casting out of Hagar and Ishmael. That took place at the time of the "great feast" which Abraham made the day Isaac was weaned (Gen. 21:8-10). This is an important event in the annals of God's people, because of its deep spiritual significance, as appears by the reference to it in Gal. 4:29-30.

From the foregoing Scriptures we are able to arrive at the date when Isaac was weaned and Ishmael was cast out (whereby Isaac became the acknowledged "seed" and "heir "). For there is a difference of thirty years between the two periods. But we have already found that there were twenty-five years from the call of Abraham (and God's "covenant" with him) to the birth of Isaac. Hence, deducting 25 from 30 gives us *5* years as the age of Isaac when Ishmael was cast out.

There is no need to give at greater length the proofs concerning the 400-year period, and the 430-year period, for all chronologers of repute, from Ussher down to the present day, arc agreed as to the chronological significance of those proofs. By one and all the date of the Exodus is given as An. Hom. 2513.

With the help of the foregoing explanations we can now construct a table of the lives of Abraham and Isaac down to the death of Abraham, and the marriage of Esau.

Table III

| | *An. Hom.* | *B.C.* |
|---|---|---|
| Birth of Abram (see preceding table) | 2008 | 2038 |
| Abram's entrance into Canaan (age 75) | 2083 | 1963 |
| Abram's marriage with Hagar (Gen. 16:3) | 2093 | 1953 |
| Ishmael born (Gen. 16:16) | 2094 | 1952 |
| Isaac promised, the everlasting covenant given, circumcision appointed, Abram's name changed to Abraham (Gen. 17); Sodom destroyed (Gen. 19) | 2107 | 1939 |
| Isaac born (Gen. 21:1-3) | 2108 | 1938 |
| Isaac weaned. Ishmael cast out | 2113 | 1933 |
| Death of Sarah (Gen. 23:1). Sarah was 90 years old when Isaac was born (Gen. 17:17) and 127 years old when she died. Hence the year of her death was | 2145 | 1901 |
| (Sarah has the distinction of being the only woman the length of whose life is given in the Bible) | | |
| Isaac married (age 40: hence 2108–40=) | 2148 | 1898 |
| Birth of Esau and Jacob (Gen. 25:26) | 2168 | 1878 |
| Abraham's death (Gen. 25:7, age 175, hence 2008, the date of his birth–175=) | 2183 | 1863 |
| Esau's marriage (age 40, Gen. 26:34) | 2208 | 1838 |

## Jacob's Hegira, Vision and Marriage

We must interrupt the table at this point in order to make the investigations and computations which are needed in order to arrive at the date of Jacob's departure to Padan Aram, and that of his marriage. Those dates are not stated in the Scripture, but they can be determined by statements made in later chapters of Genesis. Thus, we learn that Joseph was 30 years of age when he stood before Pharaoh (Gen. 41:46). Hence at the end of the seven years of plenty he was 37, and after two years of famine, when Jacob himself was 130 (Gen. 47:9), he (Joseph) was 39 years of age. Therefore, since Joseph was 39 when his father Jacob was 130, the latter was 91 at the birth of Joseph. Now Jacob had served Laban 14 years when Joseph was born (Gen. 30:25).

Therefore, Jacob was 77 (9-14) when he came to Padan Aram and entered the service of Laban.

With this information we can now proceed with our table.

Table III

| | *An. Hom.* | *B.C.* |
|---|---|---|
| Esau's marriage | 2208 | 1838 |
| Jacob goes to Padan Aram, aged 77 | 2245 | 1801 |
| Jacob marries both daughters of Laban (He served 7 years before marriage for Leah, 7 years thereafter for Rachel, his age at date of marriage being 84) | 2252 | 1794 |
| Joseph born seven years later | 2259 | 1787 |
| Jacob returned to Canaan 6 years later (Gen. 31:41) aged 97 | 2265 | 1781 |
| Joseph stands before Pharoah 24 years later, aged 30 (Gen. 41:46) | 2289 | 1757 |
| Add 7 years of plenty, Joseph 37. | 2296 | 1750 |
| Two years later Jacob goes down into Egypt, age 130 (Gen. 45:6; 47:9) | 2298 | 1748 |
| Death of Jacob 17 years later (Gen. 47:28) | 2315 | 1731 |
| Death of Joseph (he was 39 when Jacob was 130, hence 39+17=56, when Jacob died, and was 110 at the time of his own death (Gen. 50:26). Hence add 54 to 2315 and we have the date of Joseph's death | 2369 | 1677 |

This completes the chronology of the Book of Genesis, which is seen to contain a perfect and connected system of dates from the creation of Adam to the death of Joseph. It begins with Adam, a living soul in the garden of Eden, and ends with the bones of Joseph in a coffin in Egypt.

## Jacob's Family in Egypt

Concerning the number of persons who came into Egypt with Jacob there are three separate statements, each of which gives a different number.

1. In Gen. 46:26 we read, "All the souls which came with Jacob into Egypt, which came out of his loins, besides Jacob's sons' wives, all the souls were threescore and six" (66 persons). This *excludes* Jacob himself, and his wives, and the wives of his sons. It excludes also Joseph and his two sons, who were already in Egypt. It specifies only those who "came *with* Jacob" and who "came *out of his loins.*"

2. In the next verse (Gen. 46:27) we read, "All the souls *of the house of Jacob* which came into Egypt were threescore and ten (70 persons). It is evident that this difference of four persons is made up by adding to the 66 of verse 26 Jacob, Joseph, Manasseh and Ephraim. This agrees with what Moses said in Deut. 10:22, "Thy fathers went down into Egypt with threescore and ten persons."

3. In Acts 7:14 Stephen said, "Then sent Joseph and called Jacob to him and *all his kindred, threescore and fifteen souls"* (75 persons). The apostles and other Jews of their day used the Septuagint version, from which version Stephen was evidently quoting, for that version adds two sons of Manasseh and three sons of Ephraim (see Num. 26:28-37 and 1 Chr. 7:20) who are not included in the Hebrew text. The expression used by Stephen "and all his kindred" is broad enough to include these five additional persons.

# CHAPTER SIX

## Israel in the Days of Moses

The chronology of the fathers of Israel comes to a full stop at the death of Joseph. There is no record of his age at the birth of either Manasseh or Ephraim. This, however, need not be wondered at, seeing that the line of Christ does not run through Joseph but through Judah. The closing chapters of Genesis are occupied with Joseph because, in the first place, he obtained the birthright after the deposition of Reuben for his crime against his father (1 Chr. 5:1); and in the second place, Joseph shines forth as a most conspicuous type of Christ; for the Scripture exhibits him as one who, through hatred and betrayal by his brethren, was delivered to the Gentiles, was cast into prison by false accusation, was associated in his punishment with two malefactors (of whom one was saved and the other lost), and who, after *three* years, was exalted to be a prince and a saviour, to work "a great deliverance" (Gen. 45:7) for his own brethren and for the world. It is most fitting that Genesis, which contains in condensed form the entire truth and doctrine of the Bible, should thus conclude with a wonderfully bright and clear type of the Saviour of men.

But the genealogy (with which runs the *chronology) did not pass to Joseph with the birthright.* Let us carefully note the language of 1 Chr. 5:1-2:

> Now the sons of Reuben the firstborn of Israel (for he

> *was* the firstborn, but forasmuch as he defiled his father's bed *his birthright was given to the sons of Joseph,* the son of Israel; and *the genealogy is not to be reckoned after the birthright;* for Judah prevailed above his brethren, and *of him came the chief ruler;* but the birthright was Joseph's).

Thus, although Joseph, the firstborn of Rachel, received the double portion (two tribes in Israel) in place of Reuben, the firstborn of Leah, "the genealogy" did not pass to Joseph along with "the birthright," but passed to Judah according to Jacob's dying prophecy (Gen. 49:10).

Hence, in accordance with the scheme of the Bible as a whole, the chronology must be brought to, and must follow thenceforth, the line of Judah. From subsequent books of the Bible we learn that from David to Jehoiachin it does follow that line; but in the intermediate period of Moses, Joshua, and the Judges, it pursues a somewhat devious course. Nevertheless, as will be seen, the count of the years is never lost.

The line of dated events in Exodus begins with Moses. But there is *no direct statement of the length of the time between the death of Joseph and the birth of Moses.* This necessary information, however, can be derived from the 430-year and 400-year periods, to which reference has been already made. For since those periods both end with the Exodus, and since the age of Moses at the date of the Exodus is given (80 years, see Exo. 7:7), we have in those facts all the information that is required to connect the chronology of Exodus with that of Genesis. For since the Exodus and the giving of the law took place 430 years after the call of Abram, we have 2083+430, giving 2513 (An. Hom.) as the year of the Exodus. And since Moses was then 80 years old we have 2513–80=2433 as the year of the birth of Moses. And since Joseph died in the year 2369, the interval between the death of Joseph and the birth of Moses was 64 years.

Tabulating these results, we obtain the following:

Table V

| | *An. Hom.* | *B.C.* |
|---|---|---|
| Death of Joseph (see preceding table) | 2369 | 1677 |
| Birth of Moses (add 64 years) | 2433 | 1613 |
| Flight of Moses from Egypt (Ex. 2:11-15) | 2473 | 1573 |
| Birth of Caleb (see Chap. Seven) | 2474 | 1572 |
| Return of Moses; Exodus of the children of Israel from Egypt | 2513 | 1533 |

## Israel in the Wilderness

The journeyings of the Israelites in the wilderness occupied a period of forty years. For some of the important events of that period the inspired record gives not only the years, but the months and days as well. Thus, the sacrifice of the paschal lamb was on the 14th day of what became, from that time onward, the first month of the year (see Ex. 12:2); and that night, which would be the 15th, "all the hosts of the LORD went out of the land of Egypt. It is a night to be much observed unto the LORD for bringing them out from the land of Egypt; this is that night of the LORD to be observed of all the children of Israel in their generations" (Ex. 12:41-42). This is confirmed by Num. 33:3, where it is recorded that, "They departed from Rameses [in Egypt] in the first month, *on the fifteenth day of the first month; on the morrow after the passover* the children of Israel went out with a high hand in the sight of all the Egyptians."

From the Exodus to the wilderness of Sin occupied just *one month;* for "the congregation of the children of Israel came unto the wilderness of Sin, which is between Elim and Sinai on the *fifteenth day of the second month* after their departing out of the land of Egypt." Hence the experiences at Marah and Elm (Ex. 15:23-27) occurred in the first month of their journeying in the wilderness.

The second month was also eventful; for in it occurred the first giving of the manna (Ex. 16) and the smiting of the rock to bring forth water (Ex. 17); and also the refusal of Jethro, Moses' father-in-law, to accompany the Israelites, and his return to his own land (Ex. 18). That these incidents took place in the second month of the first year of the Exodus appears from the statement of Ex. 19:1, "In the *third month,* when the children of Israel were gone forth out of the land of Egypt, *the same day* came they into the wilderness of Sinai."

## The Giving of the Law

In this third month of the Exodus occurred the most momentous event in the history of the earthly people of Israel prior to the crucifixion of their Messiah.

John Lightfoot notes the interesting and instructive fact that the giving of the law is a foreshadowing of Pentecost, just as the Passover is a foreshadowing of Calvary. The interval of time was about the same; but the correspondence lies in the fact that although the law came down from heaven it could not make men submissive and obedient to God, and hence the Holy Ghost came down from heaven to write the law in the hearts of God's new covenant people, so that "the righteousness of the law might be fulfilled in us who walk not after the flesh but after the Spirit" (Rom. 5:5; Rom. 8:4). The correspondence then is between the law coming down from heaven at the beginning of the dispensation of law, and the Holy Spirit coming down from heaven at the beginning of the dispensation of grace. The law of God was the equipment of His people of old for their service and testimony; the Spirit of God is the equipment of His people now.

We have noted that the giving of the law, the Ten Commandments, which was on the third day after Moses went up unto God the first time (Ex. 19:3, 11), occurred in the third month after the Exodus. The Israelites remained at the foot of Mount Sinai 9½ months, that is, to the 1st day of the 1st month of the second year (see Ex. 40:17). The principal events of those 9 months were the giving of the "statutes" and "judgments" to Moses, together with the tables of stone, during the first period of 40 days he spent up the Mount (Ex. 21-31); the making of the golden calf by the people (Ex. 31:1-6); the breaking of the tables of stone by Moses (Ex. 32:19); the execution of judgment upon Israel by the children of Levi, as a reward for which the Levites afterwards obtained the priesthood (Ex. 32:26-28); the second 40 days spent by Moses upon the Mount, when he received the second tables of stone (Ex. 34); and the building of the Tabernacle (Ex. 35-40). Thus it will be seen that some of the most significant events in the history of the people of Israel, events which are rich in spiritual lessons, occurred in the year of the Exodus.

The whole period covered by the Book of Exodus was 144 years, 111 months, a very short period as compared with the 2369 years of the Book of Genesis. Of the nearly 145 years embraced by the Book of Exodus, about 144 years are covered in chapters 1 and 2, the events of the remaining year filling the rest of the Book.

## Dates in Leviticus

The chronology of Leviticus is very brief indeed, covering only *one month;* for the events it describes occurred between the first day of the *first* month of the second year (Ex. 40:17) and the first day of the *second* month of that same year (Num. 1:1). The historical events of the Book of Leviticus are the consecration of Aaron and his sons to the priesthood (ch. 8); and the offering by Nadab and Abihu of strange fire, and their death by fire from the Lord (ch. 10).

## Dates in Numbers

The Book of Numbers begins with a date, the 1st day of the 2nd month of the 2nd year of the era of the Exodus. On that day the Lord commanded the taking of the number of the children of Israel by their tribes (Num. 1:1-2). This enumeration was finished in 20 days; for it is recorded that "it came to pass on the *twentieth* day of the second month, in the second year, that the cloud was taken up from off the tabernacle of the testimony, and the children of Israel took their journeys out of the wilderness of Sinai" (Num. 10:11-12).

Thus the measure of the stay of the Israelites at Sinai was very nearly one year. The verse last quoted (Numb. 10:12) goes on to say, "And the cloud rested in the wilderness of Paran." Between Sinai and Paran occurred the complaints of the Israelites because of dissatisfaction with the manna (ch. 11), and the leprosy of Miriam (ch. 12).

From the wilderness of Paran, whereof Kadesh Barnea is on the north-east border, not far from Palestine, Moses sent forth the twelve spies to view the land (Num. 13:3). It is recorded in Deut. 1:3 that it is but "eleven days' journey from Horeb, by way of Mount Seir to Kadesh Barnea." Hence God was ready, as well as able, to bring His people into their promised inheritance without delay after He had given them the law, statutes and judgments they were to obey in the land. It was "because of unbelief" (Heb. 3:19) that they "could not enter in." They were in the wilderness *only one year* by God's appointment, and by their own choice. For, upon hearing the evil report of the spies, they said, "Would God we had *died in this wilderness"* (Num. 14:2); and God took them at their word, saying, "As ye have spoken in my ears, so will I do unto you; your carcasses *shall fall in this wilderness"* (Num. 14:28-29).

We now have a comparatively long interval, 37 years, 11 months, without a single dated event. It would seem as if, in this way, God emphasized His disapproval of that evil generation who "provoked" Him, and who "despised the pleasant land." For He has practically ignored the history of those years.

The next date is in Num. 20:1: "Then came the children of Israel, even the whole congregation, into the desert of Zin, in the *first month;* and the people abode in Kadesh; and Miriam died there, and was buried there." From chap. 33:36-38 we learn that this "first month" was the first month of the *40th year* of the era of the Exodus. So 38 years have passed since the last dated event.

The only recorded events of those 38 years, which the Israelites spent in the wilderness by their own choice, are the stoning of the Sabbath-breaker (Num. 15:32-36) and the rebellion of Korah, Dathan and Abiram (Num. 16). These are very significant incidents in that they serve to reveal the character of that generation. They serve also to illustrate the words of Paul in the synagogue at Antioch in Pisidia, "And about the time of forty years *suffered he their manners* in the wilderness" (Acts 13:18).

On the first day of the fifth month of that 40th year of the Exodus, Aaron died on the top of Mount Hor (Num. 20:23-29; 33:38).

## The Last Year of the Forty in the Wilderness

From the death of Aaron on the first day of the fifth month, to the beginning of Moses' last address to the children of Israel, was just *six months;* for we read in Deut. 1:3, "And it came to pass in the *fortieth year,* in the *eleventh month,* on the *first day of the month,* that Moses spake unto the children of Israel, according to all that the LORD had given him in commandment unto them."

The last year of the forty in the wilderness was, like the first year thereof, a time of important events. These have been recorded for our admonition, and they are full of instruction for the household, of faith.

In Numbers 20, between the death of Miriam and that of Aaron, three months later, we have the incident of the striking of the rock (in this case the Hebrew word means an exalted or uplifted rock, not a sunken rock as in Ex. 17:6) when God had bidden Moses and Aaron to *speak* to the rock (Num. 20:8). It would seem that Aaron was jointly at fault with Moses in this act of insubjection, and in applying to the Lord's people the opprobrious term "ye rebels" (see Mat. 5:22), for the Lord said to them both, "Because *ye* believed me not to sanctify me in the eyes of the children of Israel, therefore, *ye* shall not bring this congregation into the land which I have given them" (Num. 20:12).

Following the death of Aaron is the deeply instructive incident of the lifting up of the brazen serpent in the presence of those who were bitten by the fiery serpents, which the Lord sent among the people as a judgment for speaking against God and against Moses (Num. 21:5-9). Upon this incident the Lord Jesus based His instruction to Nicodemus, concerning the Kingdom of God, in answer to his question, "How can a man be born when he is old?" (John 3:1-18).

In the same period (between the death of Aaron and the final address of Moses on the plains of Moab) occurred also the defeat of Sihon, king of the Amorites (Num. 21:21-25), and Og the king of Bashan (Num. 21:33-35); also the interesting incident of Balaam and Balak (Num. 22-24); the apostasy of Baal-peor, and the plague brought thereby upon the people (Num. 25); the second numbering of the people, the new generation, concerning which it is written, "But among these there was not a man of them whom Moses and Aaron the priest numbered, when they numbered the children of Israel in the wilderness of Sinai, ...save Caleb the son of Jephunneb, and Joshua the son of Nun" (Num. 26:64-65); the appeal of the daughters of Zelophehad for a part in the inheritance (Num. 27); and the war of vengeance upon the Midianites (Num. 31).

Tabulating the information we have gathered concerning the 40 years in the wilderness, we obtain the following:

Table VI

| | *An. Hom.* | *B.C.* | *Month* | *Day* |
|---|---|---|---|---|
| The Exodus . . . . . . . . . . . . . . . . . . . . . . . | 2513 | 1533 | 1 | 15 |
| Arrival at Wilderness of Sin . . . . . . . . . . | 2513 | 1533 | 2 | 15 |
| Giving of the Manna and Smiting of the Rock . . . . . . . . . . . . . . . . . . . . . | 2513 | 1533 | 2 | — |
| Arrival at Sinai and giving of the Ten Commandments. . . . . . . . . . . . . | 2513 | 1533 | 3 | 15 |
| Sojourn at Sinai; Statutes and Judgments given; the golden calf; the Tables of Stone broken and renewed; and the Tabernacle built – all this occupying 9½ months, and bringing us to . . . . . . . . . . . . . . . . . . . . | 2514 | 1532 | 1 | 1 |
| The events of Leviticus bring us to the numbering of Israel . . . . . . . . . . | 2514 | 1532 | 2 | 1 |

| | *An. Hom.* | *B.C.* | *Month* | *Day* |
|---|---|---|---|---|
| Numbering finished, spies sent forth . . . | 2514 | 1532 | 2 | 20 |
| Interval of 38 years (less one month) during which the Israelites wandered in the wilderness, no events being dated until the death of Miriam . . . . . . . . . . . . | 2552 | 1494 | 1 | — |
| Death of Aaron . . . . . . . . . . . . . . . . . . . | 2552 | 1494 | 5 | 1 |
| During next six months occurred lifting up of the brazen serpent, the defeat of Sihon and Og, the incident of Balaam and Balak, the apostasy of Baal-peor, and the numbering of the new generation of Israelites. This bring us to . . . . . . . . . . . . . . . . . . . . . . | 2552 | 1494 | 11 | 1 |
| But *one man* now remains (except the two who were to enter the land) of all the males above 20 years of age who came out of Egypt — *Moses* who died . . . . . . . . . | 2552 | 1494 | 12 | — |

Moses must have died early in the 12th month of the year 2552, for there were 30 days' mourning for him on the plains of Moab (Deut. 34:8); and then followed the crossing of the Jordan "after three days" (Josh. 3:2, during which time the spies entered Jericho); "and the children of Israel encamped in Gilgal and kept the passover on the *fourteenth* day of the month" (Josh. 5:10). This would be year 2553, month 1, day 14.

The statement of Deut. 34:7 that Moses was 120 years old when he died (which means in his 120th year) enables us to check our results. For Moses was born in 2433 (see Table V). Consequently in the last month of 2552, he would be in his 120th year.

# CHAPTER SEVEN

## Chronology of Joshua and Judges

The first part of the Book of Joshua describes the various wars, beginning with the siege of Jericho (chap. 6), whereby the land was subdued. But no dates are recorded; and no information is directly given whereby the length of this period can be determined. Joshua died at the age of 110 (ch. 24:29); but this does not help us, for the date of his birth is not known.

But the needed chronological link is supplied through Caleb, the son of Jephunneh, of the tribe of Judah. We have seen that the spies were sent out the 2nd year after the Exodus, in the early fall ("at the time of the first ripe grapes," Num. 13:20). This was the year 2514, 2nd month (see Table 6). At that time Caleb was *40 years old;* for he said, "Forty years old was I when Moses the servant of the LORD sent me from Kadesh Barnea to espy out the land" (Josh. 14:7). Hence Caleb was born in the year (2514–40) 2474. At the time of the division of the land by Joshua, at the conclusion of the wars of conquest, Caleb was 85 years old; for he said at that time, "And now behold, the LORD hath kept me alive as He said, these *forty and five years,…* and now, lo, I am this day *fourscore and five years old"* (Josh. 14:10). Add 85 to 2474, and we get 2559, as the year of the division of the land after the wars of conquest. Therefore, the duration of those wars was six years (2553 to 2559).

This is as far as the chronology of the Book of Joshua carries us. The next time-note we find is in Jdg. 3:8, where it is recorded that "the children of Israel served Cushan-rishathaim *eight years.*" So the question to be answered is, how many years were there between the division of the land by Joshua, An. Hom. 2559, and the oppression of Cushan-rishathaim? This has been a very difficult problem to solve. The question is examined at great length in Dr. Anstey's work; but we are concerned rather with the answer to the question, than with the arithmetical calculations by which it has been reached.

Briefly then, the answer is deduced from the words of Jephthah who said to the king of Ammon that Israel had occupied Heshbon and her towns *three hundred years* (Jdg. 11:26).

The conquest of Heshbon was the year before the Israelites entered Canaan, or 2552. Hence the 300 years would bring us to 2852. Now the Scripture gives the various constituent periods, making up these 300 years *except* the interval concerning which we are inquiring. Hence, by deducting from 300, the total of the known constituent periods, we arrive at the length of said interval. Those periods are 1 year in the wilderness, 6 years to the division of the land, servitude under Cushan 8 years (Jdg. 3:8), rest by Othniel 40 years (Jdg. 3:11), servitude under Eglon 18 years (Jdg. 3:14), rest by Ehud 80 years (Jdg. 3:30), servitude under Jabin 20 years (Jdg. 4:3), rest by Barak 40 years (Jdg. 5:31), servitude under Midian 7 years (Jdg. 6:11), rest by Gideon 40 years (Jdg. 8:28), usurpation of Abimelech 3 years (Jdg. 9:22), judgeship of Tola 23 years (Jdg. 10:2). These total 286 years, deducting which from 300 gives 14 years as the interval between the dividing of the land by Joshua and the servitude under Cushan-rishathaim.

It is worthy of note that each of the several periods, during the course of the turbulent 300 years, in which God gave His people rest, was just 40 years, except the rest-period under Ehud, which was twice 40 years.

We must refer our readers to Mr. Anstey's work for the details of this calculation, and particularly for the proof that the judgeship of Shamgar (Jdg. 3:31) is concurrent with the servitude under Jabin, and that the judgeship of Jair (Jdg. 10:3) and the servitude under Ammon (Jdg. 10:8) are not included in Jephthah's 300 years.

We make the duration of Joshua's wars of conquest to be 6 years, instead of 7, as by Anstey; for it would appear that he inadvertently made the "second year" after the Exodus to be *two* years after (which would be the *third)* whereas it was plainly the *next year.* Thus he got the period one year too long. But this slight error is automatically compensated for by making the interval from the division of the land to Cushan's oppression a year longer (14 instead of 13 according to Anstey) so that the total count of the years is not affected.

We can now tabulate the period of Joshua-Judges.

Table VII

| | *An. Hom.* | *B.C.* |
|---|---|---|
| Entrance of Israel into Canaan (14th day, 1st month) | | |
| Add 6 years to division of the land by Joshua (Josh. 13:7-10) = . . . . . . . . . . . . . . . . . . . . . . . . | 2553 | 1493 |
| Add 14 years to oppression by Cushan (Jdg. 3:8) . . | 2559 | 1487 |
| Add 8 years of servitude under Cushan to rest by Othniel (Jdg. 3:8, 11) = . . . . . . . . . . . . . . . | 2573 | 1473 |
| Add 40 years to servitude under Eglon (Jdg. 3:11,14) = | 2581 | 1465 |
| Add 18 years to rest by Ehud (Jdg. 3:14, 30) = . . . . | 2621 | 1425 |
| Add 80 years to servitude under Jabin (Jdg. 3:30) = . | 2639 | 1407 |
| Add 20 years (which includes Shamgar's judgeship (Jdg. 3:31; 4:3) to rest by Barak = . . . . . . . | 2719 | 1327 |
| Add 40 years' rest by Barak to servitude under Midian (Jdg. 5:31) = . . . . . . . . . . . . . . . . . | 2739 | 1307 |
| Add 7 years' servitude to rest by Gideon (Jdg. 6:1; 8:28) = . . . . . . . . . . . . . . . . . . . . . . . . . | 2779 | 1267 |
| Add 40 years' rest to usurpation of Abimelech (Jdg. 8:28; 9:22) = . . . . . . . . . . . . . . . . . . . . . . | 2786 | 1260 |
| Add 3 years' usurpation (Jdg. 9:22) to judgeship of Tola (Jdg. 10:2) = . . . . . . . . . . . . . . . . . . . | 2826 | 1220 |
| Add 23 years Tola to judgeship of Jair (Jdg. 10:2-3) = | 2829 | 1217 |

| | *An. Hom.* | *B.C.* |
|---|---|---|
| Add 22 years (Jdg. 10:3) to servitude under Ammon (Jdg. 10:8) = . . . . . . . . . . . . . . . . . . . . . . . . | 2874 | 1172 |
| Add 18 years of oppression (Jdg. 10:8) to the judgeship of Jephthah = . . . . . . . . . . . . . . . | 2892 | 1154 |
| Add 6 years to Ibzan (Jdg. 12:7) = . . . . . . . . . . . . . | 2898 | 1148 |
| Add 7 years to Elon (Jdg. 12:8, 11) = . . . . . . . . . . . | 2905 | 1141 |
| Add 10 years to Abdon (Jdg. 12:11, 14) = . . . . . . . . | 2915 | 1131 |
| Add 8 years to servitude under Philistines (Jdg. 12:14) = . . . . . . . . . . . . . . . . . . . . . . . . . . . | 2923 | 1123 |
| Add 40 years' servitude (Jdg. 13:1) which includes the 20 years of Samson's judgeship (Jdg. 16:31) to Eli = . . . . . . . . . . . . . . . . . . . . . . | 2963 | 1083 |
| Add 40 years Eli's judgeship (1 Sam. 4:18) to Samuel = . . . . . . . . . . . . . . . . . . . . . . . . . . | 3003 | 1043 |
| Add 20 years Samuel's judgeship (1 Sam. 7:2) to Saul = . . . . . . . . . . . . . . . . . . . . . . . . . . . . | 3023 | 1023 |

## The 450 Years of Paul (Acts 13:20)

In connection with the period now under consideration attention should be given to the statement of the apostle Paul in addressing those gathered in the synagogue at Antioch in Pisidia (Asia Minor). He said, "And about the time of forty years suffered he their manners in the wilderness. And when he had destroyed seven nations in the land of Canaan, he divided their land to them by lot. And after that, he gave unto them judges about the space of *four hundred and fifty years,* until Samuel the prophet" (Acts 13:18-20).

This epoch of 450 years, the period of the Judges, appears to be made up in the following way. By examining details of Table VII it will be found that, if the several periods, beginning with the 8 years' servitude under Cushan, and ending with the 20 years' judgeship of Samuel, be added together, they make up a total of just 450 years. It is reasonable, therefore, to infer that this is the period spoken of by the apostle; and on the other hand it is warrantable to take his statement as a confirmation of the conclusions stated above, and summarized in Table VII, in which we have followed Anstey.

## The 480 Years of 1 Kings 6:1

Great difficulty to chronologists has been occasioned by the statement of 1 Kgs. 6:1, which says that the beginning of the building of the temple in the 4th year of King Solomon was "in the four hundred and eightieth year after the children of Israel were come out of the land of Egypt."

The total of the years taken in detail, from the Exodus to the 4th year of Solomon, is 594, an excess of 114 years over the statement of 1 Kgs. 6:1. This raises one of the most difficult chronological problems of the Bible. Some chronologers, as Jackson, Clinton, and Hales, reject the statement of 1 Kgs. 6:1 as an interpolation, because manifestly contradicted by the detailed chronology of the Scriptures. But Bishop Ussher (whose dates are incorporated in the margin of some editions of the Bible) adopts it without qualification, making the length of the period in question 480 years, instead of 594. To bring this about, he abridges the period from the entrance into the land to the reign of Saul, by taking off some years at one place and some at another. For example, he changes the rest by Ehud from "fourscore years" (Jdg. 3:30) to 20, and so on. Manifestly this affects, to the extent of 114 years, *every previous date expressed in terms "B. C.," and all subsequent dates expressed in terms "An. Hom." or "A.M."*

Dr. Anstey, however, calls attention to the striking fact that the discrepancy "114 years" is *exactly the measure of the six servitudes and the one usurpation* which interrupt the period of God's government of His people through the Judges; and Dr. Anstey suggests that the 480 years are put down as the measure of the Theocracy (God's rule over His people), and that the years when God gave over the rule of His people to their enemies are not reckoned in the statement of 1 Kgs. 6:1. This we accept as the best available explanation of the difficulty. But, in any case, the detailed chronology, derived by putting together the several statements of Scripture, must be maintained.

The period covered by Table VII is one of much confusion in Israel, and of departure from the statutes and judgments which God had given His people to walk in. "There was no king in Israel" in those days, and hence "every man did that which was right in his own eyes" (Jdg. 17:6; Jdg. 18:1, &c.). It would seem as if, on this account, it were a matter of unusual difficulty to trace the workings of the hand of God in the affairs of His people, and that the chronology is, in consequence, relatively obscure. In regard to no other part of the Bible is there a greater lack of unanimity amongst chronologers of repute.

# CHAPTER EIGHT

## King Saul

The annals of the reign of Saul are almost destitute of chronological information. In fact it is doubtful if the length of Saul's reign could be determined but for the statement of the apostle Paul in Acts 13:21, "And afterward they desired a king; and God gave unto them Saul, the son of Cis, a man of the tribe of Benjamin, by the space of *forty years.*"

The only statement of a chronological character in the Old Testament concerning Saul is one so remarkable that it has been quite a puzzle to chronologers. It is found in 1 Sam. 13:1-2. As rendered in the A.V. it reads: "Saul reigned one year; and when he had reigned two years over Israel, Saul chose him two thousand men of Israel," etc. The margin tells us that the words "reigned one year" read in the original Hebrew "the son of one year in his reigning." There is, however, a disagreement as to the text, which is rendered in some versions, "Saul was — years when he began to reign, and when he had reigned two years," etc. So we dismiss this passage as being of no importance for our present purposes, it being enough to know, from Acts 13:21, that the reign of Saul lasted 40 years.

## David and Solomon

David and Solomon each reigned 40 years. We would judge that to be the normal length of the reign of a ruler; for 40 appears to be the Bible-number of a full period of testing or probation, instance the forty years of the Israelites in the wilderness, the forty days of the Lord's trial in the wilderness, etc. There is something significant in the fact that each of the first three kings of Israel, the only three who reigned over a *united* kingdom, reigned each for 40 years. Of David it is recorded that "David was thirty years old when he began to reign, and he reigned forty years. In Hebron he reigned over Judah seven years and six months; and in Jerusalem he reigned thirty and three years over all Israel and Judah" (2 Sam. 5:4-5). During the time David reigned over Judah only, Ishbosheth, the son of Saul, reigned two years over Israel (2 Sam. 2:10). These two periods make a total of 40½ years; but when reduced to *calendar* years they figure 40 years.

The length of Solomon's reign is stated in 2 Chr. 9:30, "And Solomon reigned in Jerusalem over all Israel *forty years.*"

These were typical reigns. In Saul we have the trial of the *natural man;* and though his unfitness to rule was quickly manifested, yet God permitted him to fill out his full term. This suggests God's long patience and forbearance with the natural man, giving him full opportunity to prove his worth in every capacity.

As regards the ideal "governor," we could have no better description than that given in the last words of David, "He that ruleth over men must be just, ruling in the fear of God" (2 Sam. 23:3). The natural man cannot meet this test. Indeed none can fully measure up to it save the Lord Jesus Christ Himself.

David and Solomon are both typical of Christ as King. The former foreshadows Christ in His rejection and conflicts; the latter foreshadows His reign of peace and glory, when He shall have put all enemies under His feet (1 Cor. 15:25). To each God gave a full measure of time. Hence the fitness in the type of a reign of forty years to each of those kings.

During David's reign the materials for the building of the temple were prepared. During Solomon's reign the Temple was completed in all its marvelous beauty and glory. This suggests the fact that now, during the time of conflict with the enemies of God, the materials for the Church are being gathered and made ready; and in the coming day it will be manifested with Christ in glory.

The dated events of Solomon's reign are the beginning of the temple in his fourth year (2 Chr. 3:2); its completion in the eleventh year (1 Kgs. 6:38, "so he was seven years in building it"); the beginning of his own house in the eleventh year, and its completion in the 24th year (1 Kgs. 7:1, 9:10).

This gives us, for the time Israel existed as a united kingdom, the following:

Table VIII

| | *An. Hom.* | *B.C.* |
|---|---|---|
| Beginning of Saul's reign (see Table VII) . . . . . . . . | 3023 | 1023 |
| Beginning of David's reign . . . . . . . . . . . . . . . . . . . | 3063 | 983 |
| Beginning of Solomon's reign . . . . . . . . . . . . . . . . . | 3103 | 943 |
| Death of Solomon . . . . . . . . . . . . . . . . . . . . . . . . . | 3143 | 903 |

## The Divided Kingdom

We come now to a portion of Scripture, Kings and Chronicles, where difficulties abound, and where the utmost care, patience, and penetration are required, in order to elucidate the facts pertaining to chronology. But the ground has been carefully explored, and the evidences scrutinized by able men in by-gone days; so that our own task is the comparatively easy one of setting forth, in a manner as simple as possible, the results of their fruitful labours. Dr. Anstey, speaking of the period of the kings of Israel and Judah, says, "There is not a single difficulty that has been raised which is not capable of a simple and easy solution, without doing violence to the text; there is not a single difficulty that has not been satisfactorily cleared up in standard works by able chronologers, from *The Chronicle of the Events of the Old Testament,* by Dr. John Lightfoot, in the 17th century, down to our own day."

Dr. John Lightfoot, to whom Anstey refers, makes some quaint observations, which give a good idea of the difficulties in question, and also of the spirit in which he, and other men of God, undertook the solution of them.

> In casting up the times of the collateral kingdoms, your only way is to lay them in two columns, one justly paralleling the other, and run them both by years as the text directs you. But here nicety is needed not to see how strangely they are reckoned, sometimes inclusive, sometimes otherwise (for this you will easily find) but to *find a reason why they be so reckoned.* Rehoboam's years are counted complete; Abijam's are current. Whereas it is said that Jeroboam reigned 22 years, and his son Nadab 2 years, you will find by this reckoning that Nadab's 2 years fall within the sum of his father's 22. This may seem strange; but the solution is sweet and easy from 2 Chr. 13:20. The Lord smote Jeroboam with some ill disease, that he could not administer or rule the kingdom, so that he was forced to substitute Nadab *in his own lifetime.* And in one and the same year, both father and son die.

The passage to which Lightfoot here refers as giving the simple solution of this seeming contradiction, reads thus: "Neither did Jeroboam recover strength again in the days of Abijah; and the LORD struck him, and he died."

There were other instances then, as has commonly happened since, that a son has ascended the throne *during his father's lifetime.* In such cases the years of their joint reigns would be reckoned to the reign of each. This is a point for which chronologers have to be continually on the lookout; but the knowledge of it enables many difficulties to be cleared up.

Continuing, Dr. Lightfoot says:

> Divers such passages as these you will find in this story of the Kings. Ahaziah two years older than his father (2 Chr. 22:2); Baasha fighting nine years after he was dead (2 Chr. 16:1); Jotham reigning four years after he was buried (2 Kgs. 15:30); Joram crowned king in the 17th year of Jehoshaphat (according to 2 Kgs. 1:17 with 1 Kgs. 22: 51), and in the 22nd year of Jehoshaphat (according to 2 Kgs. 8:16), and after Jeshoshaphat's death (2 Chr. 21:1).
>
> For the resolution of such ambiguities, the text will do

> it, *if it be well searched.* This way, attained to, will guide you in marking those things that seem to be contradictions in the text, or slips of the Holy Ghost, in which always is admirable wisdom.
>
> Admirable it is to see how the Holy Spirit of God hath, in discords, showed the sweet music. But few mark this, because few take a right course in the reading of Scripture. Hence, when men are brought to see flat contradictions (as, unreconciled, there be many in it) they are at amaze, and ready to deny their Bible. A little pains, right spent, will soon amend this wavering, and settle men upon the rock whereon to be built is to be sure.

Dr. Anstey refers to an article by Willis J. Beecher on "The Kings of Israel and Judah," in the *American Presbyterian Review* for April, 1880, as giving "the key to the solution of all these difficulties." We quote some of the rules given by Mr. Beecher, and which, according to Anstey, "are obeyed with entire uniformity in all the dates of the period under consideration."

> *Rule 1.* All the years mentioned are current years of a consecutive system. The first year of a king is, not a year's time *beginning with the day and month of his accession,* but, a year's time beginning with (1) *the preceding,* or (2) *the following New Year's Day* i.e., the New Moon before the Passover, Nisan 1st.
>
> *Rule 2.* When a reign closes and another begins during a year, that year is counted to the previous reign (Judaite mode).
>
> *Rule 3.* Regularly in the case of the earlier kings of Israel, and occasionally in other cases, the broken year is counted to *the following reign,* as well as to *the previous reign* (Israelite mode).

Concerning the history of the period of the divided kingdom, Dr. Anstey says:

> The Hebrew text of the history of this period is self-consistent and self-contained. All the data required for the resolution of any difficulties that may arise are to be found *in the text itself.* There is no need to fall back upon Josephus. Still less is there any need to introduce any of the harmonizing expedients of the LXX, or any of the "emendations," "restorations," and "correc-

tions" of the text by modern critics, who present us with a view of the history as *they* think it *ought* to be, not with a view of the history *as it is.*

Similarly, the use of "Sothic Cycles," the calculation of eclipses, and other astronomical methods and expedients for settling Bible dates, are all alike inadmissible. They are liable, first, to errors of *observation* on the part of the original observer; second, to errors of *calculation* on the part of the modem astronomer; and consequently, third, to errors in the *identification* of the observed and recorded eclipse with the eclipse reached by calculation. Those methods are used mainly in support of assumptions and pre-suppositions already arrived at by hypothesis and conjecture. They may be true or they may not. But in any case, they cannot be erected into a standard by which to correct the data given in the Hebrew text. Modern Egyptologists make much of astronomical data. Each advocate regards his own scheme as thereby invested with the certainty of a mathematical calculation. But there are *many such schemes,* and they differ from each other *by more than a century.* As Willis J. Beecher says, "Each chain has links of the solid steel of astronomical computations, but they are tied together with the rotten twine of conjecture."

The quasi-infallible dates arrived at by modern investigators are erected into a standard by which to amend and correct the dates of the Hebrew text of the Old Testament. But this is correcting standard coin of the realm by means of counterfeit fabrications. For the authentic documents of the Hebrew Old Testament are both accurate, complete, and self-sufficient. The fact and the events, the dates and the periods, there given, are as accurate and as much to be relied upon as are those other statements upon which we base our confidence in the goodness of God, and rest in hope of eternal salvation.

# CHAPTER NINE

## The Chronology of the Divided Kingdom to the Accession of Jehu

We now give a table exhibiting the contemporary reigns of the kings of Judah and Israel, and events which are dated in the Bible, from the death of Solomon, An. Hom. 3143, where our last table ended, down to the death of Ahaziah of Judah and Jehoram of Israel, both which kings were slain by Jehu in the same year (An. Hom. 3232).

The year of the death of Solomon was the year of Rehoboam's accession to the throne of Judah, and of Jeroboam's accession to the throne of Israel. Following this table we will give some explanations (where such are needed) of the passages of Scripture from which the chronological facts are taken.

Table IX

*The Contemporary Kingdoms of Judah and Israel From the Death of Solomon to That of Ahaziah of Judah*

(Where a king's name appears for the first time it is the year of his accession to the throne).

| *Events* | *Judah* | *Israel* | *A.H.* | *B.C.* |
|---|---|---|---|---|
| Death of Solomon. Disruption of the kingdom. Ten tribes revolt and set up an independent kingdom under Jeroboam (1 Kgs. 12:19-20). Rehoboam reigned 17 years (1 Kgs. 14:21). For the first three years he walked in the ways of David (2 Chr. 11:17). | Rehoboam | Jeroboam | 3143 | 903 |
| In the 5th year of his reign Shishak, king of Egypt, plundered the Temple (1 Kgs. 14:25). | | | 3147 | 899 |
| Rehoboan died. | | | 3159 | 887 |
| Abijam reigned in the 18th year of Jeroboam, 3 years (1 Kgs. 15:1-2). | Abijam | | 3160 | 886 |
| Abijam dies, succeeded by Asa (1 Kgs. 15:9). | Asa | | 3162 | 884 |
| Nadab reigned over Israel the 2nd year of Asa (1 Kgs. 15:25). | | Nadab | 3164 | 882 |
| Baasha reigned the 3rd year of Asa (1 Kgs. 15:28, 33). | | Baasha | 3165 | 881 |
| Great religious revival in Asa's reign under the prophesying of Azariah and Obed (2 Chr. 15:1-10) Asa's 15th year. | | | 3177 | 869 |
| Baasha invades Judah (2 Chr. 16:1; see explanation below). | | | 3178 | 868 |
| Elah, son of Baasha, reigned the 26th year of Asa, 2 years (1 Kgs. 16:8). | | Elah | 3188 | 858 |
| Zimri slew Elah, in fulfillment of the Word of the Lord (1 Kgs. 16:3, 9, 10), and is in | | | | |

| *Events* | *Judah* | *Israel* | *A. H.* | *B.C.* |
|---|---|---|---|---|
| turn slain by Omri the same year, Omri and Tibni reigning concurrently as rival kings. | | Zimri<br>Omri<br>Tibni | 3189 | 857 |
| Tibni died. Omri continued to reign in the 31st year of Asa (1 Kgs. 16:22-23). | | | 3193 | 853 |
| Omri bought the hill of Samaria, built a city there, and made it the capital of his kingdom (1 Kgs. 16:23-24). | | | 3194 | 852 |
| Ahab succeeds Omri in the 38th of Asa (1 Kgs. 16:29). | | Ahab | 3200 | 846 |
| Asa diseased in his feet (2 Chr. 16:12). | | | 3201 | 845 |
| Asa dies, Jehoshaphat succeeds him (2 Chr. 16:13; 1 Kgs. 22:41-42). | Jehoshaphat | | 3203 | 843 |
| Jehoshaphat, in his third year, sent forth princes and priests to teach the Book of the Law in the cities of Judah (2 Chr. 17:7-9). | | | 3206 | 840 |
| Ahab slain in battle with the Syrians, Ahaziah, his son, succeeds him (1 Kgs. 22:37-40, 51), 17th year of Jehoshaphat, and reigned two years. | | Ahaziah | 3220 | 826 |
| Jehoram reigns *for* Jehoshaphat (see 2 Kgs. 1:17 with 3:1). | Jehoram (pro-rex) | | 3220 | 826 |
| Elijah calls fire from heaven, destroying two captains and their companions (2 Kgs. 1:9-12). Ahaziah of Israel dies, succeeded by Jehoram, in second year of Jeho- | | | | |

| *Events* | *Judah* | *Israel* | *A. H.* | *B.C.* |
|---|---|---|---|---|
| ram of Judah (2 Kgs. 1:17; 3:1). | | Jehoram | 3221 | 825 |
| Jehoram of Judah reigns *with* Jehoshaphat as co-rex (2 Kgs. 8:16-17). | Jehoram as co-rex | | 3225 | 821 |
| Jehoshaphat dies, and Jehoram reigns (now as *sole* king, 1 Kgs. 22:50). | Jehoram as sole king | | 3229 | 817 |
| Ahaziah begins to reign (jointly with his father) in 11th year of Jehoram of Israel (2 Kgs. 9:29). | Ahaziah as co-rex | | 3231 | 815 |
| Ahaziah one year as sole king (2 Kgs. 8:25-26). | Ahaziah as sole king | | 3232 | 814 |
| Ahaziah of Judah and Jehoram of Israel both slain by Jehu. Former succeeded by queen Athaliah, latter by Jehu (2 Kgs. 9:13-33; 10:36; 2 Kgs. 11:1-4). | | | 3232 | 814 |

Some explanations are required to make the foregoing table clear.

## Baasha's Invasion of Judah

In 2 Chr. 16:1-3 it is stated that "in the six and thirtieth year of the reign of Asa, Baasha, king of Israel, came up against Judah." But the 36th year of Asa would be *nine years after the death of Baasha,* this being what Lightfoot referred to in speaking of "Baasha fighting nine years after he was dead." The Hebrew text, however, says, not that it was the 36th year of the *reign* of Asa, as in our A. V., but that it was the 36th year of the *kingdom* of Asa. So it is evident that the reckoning here is from the beginning of the *separate kingdom* of Judah. Hence the invasion of Judah by Baasha would be in the 16th year of Asa, and the 13th of his own reign, as tabulated above.

## Apparent Contradictions as to Jehoram

Again there is apparent disagreement or contradiction in regard to the beginning of the reign of Jehoram, son of Jehoshaphat, king of Judah. According to 1 Kgs. 22:41, 50, Jehoshaphat reigned 25 years, and was succeeded by Jehoram. This would make the beginning of the latter's reign in the year 3228. But, according to 2 Kgs. 1:17, Jehoram of Judah had been already reigning one year when Jehoram of Israel succeeded his father Ahab, which was in the year 3221. Again, in 2 Kgs. 3:1 it is stated that Jehoram the son of Ahab "began to reign over Israel the *eighteenth year of Jehoshaphat,* king of Judah." Thus, Jehoram of Israel began to reign in the 18th year of Jehoshaphat, and in the 2nd year of Jehoram his son. Evidently then, Jehoram was at that time reigning *in the place* of his father, Jehoshaphat, either because of some disability, or for other reason, not stated. Such incidents have often occurred. In the margin of the Cambridge Bible is the following note on 2 Kgs. 1:17, which explains the matter: "The second year that Jehoram was *pro-rex,* and the eighteenth year of Jehoshaphat: ch. 3:1."

Again in 2 Kgs. 8:16 we find the following record: "And in the fifth year of Joram, the son of Ahab, king of Israel, *Jehoshaphat being then king of Judah,* Jehoram, the son of Jehoshaphat, king of Judah, began to reign." Here is a plain statement that Jehoram reigned *at the same time* with his father Jehoshaphat. Accordingly his name appears on the table as co-rex. The words "began to reign" should be simply "reigned" (see margin). In fact Jehoram *began* to reign, as we have seen, five years previously.

Finally, Jehoram's reign as *sole* king began at the death of his father, after the latter had reigned 25 years (1 Kgs. 22:41, 50).

Thus the seeming contradiction as to the three several beginnings of Jehoram's reign is clearly explained. Those who wish a more complete and detailed explanation will find it in Dr. Anstey's work.

## How the Accuracy of the Record is Insured

In regard to this period of Bible history, and the way the succession of the several kings is recorded, we quote some helpful observations of Dr. Anstey:

> The reigns of the kings of the first two periods are so locked and interlocked that it is impossible for any error to have crept into the chronology between the year of the disruption and the year of the fall of Samaria.
>
> The accuracy of the chronology of the kingdom of Judah from the fall of Samaria to the captivity is likewise guaranteed, being checked by' the long numbers which measure the intervals between two distant events, e.g., the period from the 13th of Josiah, when the ministry of Jeremiah began, to the 4th year of Jehoiakim, which is given as a period of 23 years (Jer. 25:1-3).

Another point which must be kept in mind in order that the details of the chronology may be understood is that the same year is often *counted twice,* being allotted both to the reign of the deceased king, and also to that of the king who succeeds him. This is the common practice in reckoning the succession of the kings of Israel, but not that of the kings of Judah. We give the explanation of this point also in the words of Dr. Anstey:

> Scripture chronology deals only with integral years. It reckons a broken year sometimes as one whole year which it gives to the outgoing king, and sometimes as two whole years, of which it gives one to the outgoing and one to the incoming king, the year being thus reckoned twice over. It follows from this fact that the chronology of the period cannot be ascertained by applying the process of simple addition to the figures denoting the lengths of the reigns of the various kings. This is easily demonstrated.
>
> In the first period the sum of the reigns of the six kings of Judah, Rehoboam to Ahaziah, is 95 years. The sum of the reigns of the 9 kings of Israel, from Jeroboam to Jehoram, is 98 years. But the true chronology of the period is 90 years. The ex-

planation of the discrepancy lies in the fact that in the figures 95 and 98 some years have been reckoned twice over.

In the second period the sum of the reigns of the 6 kings and 1 queen of Judah, from Athaliah to the 6th year of Hezekiah, including the interregnum of 11 years, is 176 years. The sum of the reigns of the 10 kings of Israel from Jehu to Hoshea, including the interregnums of 22 and 8 years respectively, is 175 years, reckoning a full year each to Zechariah and Shallum. The true chronology of the period, however, is 174 years, and the explanation of the discrepancy is the same as before.

In the third period, the sum of the reigns of the six kings of Judah, from the 6th year of Hezekiah to the 3rd year of Jehoiakim, is 114. The true chronology of the period is also 114 years.

## Jehoshaphat and His Affiliations with Ahab

Jehoshaphat was one of the good kings of Judah; for it is recorded of him that "the LORD was with Jehoshaphat, because he walked in the first ways of his father David" (2 Chr. 17:3); and further that, in the *third year* of his reign, he sent forth princes, priests and Levites, throughout all the cities of Judah, with the Book of the Law, to teach the people. God accordingly recompensed the fidelity of His servant, during that period of his reign, in that the fear of the Lord was upon all the kingdoms round about Judah, so that they made no war against Jehoshaphat (2 Chr. 17:7-10).

But, after certain years, Jehoshaphat "joined affinity with Ahab," who was the worst of all the bad kings of Israel (see 1 Kgs. 16:30-34); and from that time onward the record of his reign is largely one of wars and other troubles. The history of Jehoshaphat seems, therefore, to have been written for the special purpose of showing what evil consequences may be expected to follow when one of the people of God "joins affinity with," that is to say, enters into intimate relations or makes common cause with, the ungodly.

We have only to look at the chronological table (Table IX) to see the results of this misstep on the part of King Jehoshaphat. Instead of a clear separation from the ungodly king of Israel and his wicked queen Jezebel, there are plain marks of intimacy, in that the same names, *Ahaziah* and *Jehoram,* appear in both the royal families. Apparently Jehoshaphat named a son after Ahab's first born, Ahaziah, and Ahab reciprocally named a son after Jehoshaphat's first born, Jehoram. And not only so, but Jehoram (of Judah) "had the daughter of Ahab to wife" (2 Chr. 21:6) and the consequence was that he exceeded all the kings of Judah in wickedness; for he slew all his own brethren; he made high places in the mountains of Judah; and he walked in the ways of the house of Ahab, introducing the licentious worship of Baal, and even compelling the people of Judah to commit fornication (2 Chr. 21:4-13). Therefore the Lord smote the people with a great plague; and smote Jehoram himself with a loathsome disease, wherewith he was afflicted for two years, until his bowels fell out by reason of his sickness, and he died of sore diseases.

It is evident that Ahaziah, son of Jehoram of Judah, began to reign as co-rex with his father during the last two years of his (Jehoram's) reign, and doubtless because of his very serious illness. For it is stated in 2 Kgs. 9:29 that "in the *eleventh* year of Joram, the son of Ahab, began Ahaziah to reign over Judah." This would be the year 3231, as shown in Table IX. But we read in 2 Kgs. 8:25-26, that Ahaziah began to reign in the *twelfth* year of Joram, and reigned *one year,* from which it appears that the reference here is to the beginning of his reign as *sole* king, after the death of his father, Jehoram. That same year he paid a visit to his uncle Jehoram of Israel (his mother's brother) when the latter was sick by reason of wounds received in battle with the Syrians (2 Kgs. 8:28-29).

## The Seeming Contradiction Concerning the Age of Ahaziah

This Ahaziah of Judah is the king whose age, as given in 2 Chr. 22:2, makes him out to be older than his own father (see the remarks of Dr. John Lightfoot, quoted above). Yet there is, as Lightfoot said, "admirable wisdom" in these seeming "slips of the Holy Ghost"; and "sweet music" for the anointed ear, where another would find "discords." For on the face of the two passages there is a plain contradiction. In 2 Kgs. 8:26 it is recorded that, *"Two and twenty* years old was Ahaziah when he began to reign"; whereas in 2 Chr. 22:2 we read, *"Forty and two* years old was Ahaziah when he began to reign."

Dr. Anstey gives two rules for solving this and like difficulties: "First, look to the original Hebrew; and second, read carefully the context." In this case he gives the literal translation of 2 Chr. 22:2, as follows: *"A son of 42 years* was Ahaziah when he began to reign." What meaning do we gather from the peculiar words, "a son of 42 years"? The first year of Ahaziah was 3231 (see Table IX). Counting back 42 years brings us to 3186 which (see Table IX again) was the year that Omri, Azariah's great grandfather, *on his mother's side* (Athaliah, daughter of Ahab), founded the new dynasty, whereof Azariah of Judah was an offshoot. "So that," to quote Anstey, "just as the sacred writer reckons the years of the kingdom of Asa from the true origin of the separated kingdom of Judah (2 Chr. 16:1), so here he reckons the years of Ahaziah from the accession of the dynasty of Omri.

And why this unusual mode of reckoning? For answer we follow the second rule laid down above, and look to the context. The complete translation of 2 Chr. 22:2-9, as given by Anstey, is as follows:

> A son of 42 years was Ahaziah when he began to reign; and he reigned one year in Jerusalem, and his mother's name was *Athaliah, the daughter of Omri. He also walked in the ways of the house of Ahab. He did evil like the house of Ahab.* And the destruction of Ahaziah was of God by his coming to Joram. For he went out with Joram against Jehu, whom the Lord had anointed to cut off the house of Ahab. And when Jehu was executing judgment upon the house of Ahab, and found the princes of Judah and the sons of the brethren of Ahaziah, he slew them. And he sought Ahaziah; and they caught him (for he was hid in Samaria) and when they had slain him, they buried him; for they

> said, He is the son of Jehoshaphat, who sought the Lord with all his heart.

The inference from this is that, in making up the Book of Chronicles, which has a different purpose from that of Kings, being the record of the house of David *in connection with the building and the maintenance of the Temple,* Ahaziah is not counted as a son of David's line at all. As Anstey says:

> He is the son of *Athaliah,* the daughter of *Ahab* and *Jezebel.* He is *no seed of David.* He is an imp of the house of Ahab, a son of the house of Omri, and as such he is "a son of 42 years"; for the dynasty of the house of Omri was *exactly* 42 *years old.* That is not the "modern" way of writing history, but it is the way of the Old Testament writers; and if we wish to understand their writings, we must put ourselves at their point of view, and not force our meaning upon their words.
>
> This interpretation is confirmed by St. Matthew, who will have it that... Jehoshaphat begat Jehoram, but *not that Jehoram begat Ahaziah, or Joash, or Amaziah – but* only the fourth in the line of descent "Jehoram begat Uzziah," his great-great-grandson. "Let the posterity of the wicked be cut off, and in the generation following let their name be blotted out" (Psa. 109:13).

## Elijah and Elisha

The reign of Ahab was distinguished by the ministry of those great prophets, Elijah and Elisha, wherein was given a conspicuous manifestation of the faithfulness and the grace of God. Wickedness was at its very height in Israel. But when the enemy comes in like a flood, then the Spirit of the Lord raises a standard against him (Isa. 59:19). There were some thousands in Israel who refused to follow in the ways of Ahab; and therefore the Lord raised up the two great prophets to bear a testimony to His Name in those days of almost total corruption and apostasy.

## Vengeance Executed by Jehu

This dark period was brought to a bloody end by a ministry of judgment executed by the hand of Jehu. He made a thorough work of it, slaying Joram (Jehoram) and his mother Jezebel (2 Kgs. 9:21-37), and the seventy sons of Ahab (10:1-7) and "all that remained of the house of Ahab in Jezreel, and all his great men and his kinsfolks and his priests, until he left him none remaining" (10:11). Moreover, "when he came to Samaria, he slew all that remained unto Ahab in Samaria, till he had destroyed him, according to the saying of the LORD which He spake to Elijah" (10:17). And finally, he executed the vengeance of God upon the priests and worshippers of Baal (10:19-27). Moreover, because of the intimacy between Ahaziah, king of Judah, and the house of Ahab, the former also was involved in the extermination of the latter, for Ahaziah was slain at the same time with his uncle, Jehoram of Israel (2 Kgs. 9:27). In 2 Chr. 22:7-9 it is recorded that "the destruction of Ahaziah *was of God* by coming to Joram; for when he was come he went out with Jehoram against Jehu the son of Nimshi, whom the LORD had anointed to cut off the house of Ahab. And it came to pass that when Jehu was executing judgment upon the house of Ahab and found the princes of Judah, and the sons of the brethren of Ahaziah, ...he slew them. And he sought Ahaziah; and they caught him (for he was hid in Samaria) and brought him to Jehu. And when they had slain him they buried him."

## The Miraculous Preservation of the House and Lineage of David

This execution of the wrath of God by Jehu marks a distinct epoch in the history of the two concurrent kingdoms of Judah and Israel, in that both thrones became vacant at the same time, and by reason of the same execution of the righteous judgment of God. Jehu succeeded to the throne of Israel; but there was more trouble and humiliation for Judah. For "when Athaliah the mother of Ahaziah saw that her son was dead, she arose and destroyed all the seed royal of the house of Judah." Thus the extermination of the house of David would have been as complete as that of the house of Ahab; but that Jehoshabeath, the daughter of the king, stole Joash, the infant son of Ahaziah, and hid him from Athaliah, so that she slew him not (2 Chr. 22:11-12).

Thus the second period of the divided kingdom begins with the fierce and impetuous Jehu on the throne of Israel, and with a woman, *a daughter of the house of Ahab,* ruling over Judah. Such were some of the consequences of Jehoshaphat's intimacy with the wicked king of Israel.

# CHAPTER TEN

## Second Period to the Fall of Samaria

The second period of the divided kingdom extends from the beginning of Jehu's reign over the northern kingdom to the fall of Samaria (the end of that kingdom), which was in the 6th year of Hezekiah, king of Judah. The principal dated events of this period appear on the following table:

Table X

| *Events* | *Judah* | *Israel* | *A.H.* | *B.C.* |
|---|---|---|---|---|
| Accession of Athaliah and Jehu (see preceding table). | Athaliah | Jehu | 3232 | 814 |
| Athaliah reigned 6 years and in the seventh year she was slain, and was succeeded by Joash (called in 2 Kgs. 12:1 Jehoash; 2 Kgs. 11:4-16). | Joash | | 3239 | 807 |
| Jehu reigned 28 years (2 Kgs. 10:36) and was succeeded by his son, Jehoahaz, in the 23rd year of Joash (2 Kgs. 13:1). | | Jehoahaz | 3261 | 785 |
| In this same year Joash stirred up the priests to repair the Temple (2 Kgs. 12:6-7). | | | 3261 | 785 |

| *Events* | *Judah* | *Israel* | *A.H.* | *B.C.* |
|---|---|---|---|---|
| In the 37th year of Joash began Jehoash to reign in Israel (as co-rex with Jehoahaz; 2 Kgs. 13:9-10). | | Jehoash (co-rex) | 3275 | 771 |
| In the 40th year of Joash, Jehoahaz, king of Israel, died and Jehoash reigned as sole king (2 Kgs. 13:9-10). | | Jehoash (sole king) | 3278 | 768 |
| Amaziah succeeded his father Joash as king of Judah in the 2nd year of Jehoash of Israel (2 Kgs. 12:21; 14:1-2). | Amaziah | | 3279 | 767 |
| In the 15th year of Amaziah, Jeroboam II reigned as king of Israel (2 Kgs. 14:16, 23). He reigned 41 years. | | Jeroboam II | 3293 | 753 |
| Amaziah, king of Judah, lived after the death of Jehoash, king of Israel, fifteen years (2 Kgs. 14:17), died. | | | 3308 | 738 |
| Amaziah had no immediate successor, for Uzziah did not come to the throne until the 27th year of Jeroboam II. Hence an Interregnum for eleven years. | Interregnum | | 3308 | 738 |
| Uzziah (Azariah) begins to reign in the 27th year of Jeroboam II (2 Kgs. 14:21; 15:1-2). | Uzziah (or Azariah) | | 3319 | 727 |
| Following the 41st year of Jeroboam II, the throne of Israel was evidently vacant for 22 years, for Zechariah did not ascend the throne until Uzziah's 38th year (2 Kgs. 14:29; 15:8). | | Interregnum | 3334 | 712 |

| *Events* | *Judah* | *Israel* | *A.H.* | *B.C.* |
|---|---|---|---|---|
| Zechariah reigns 6 months in Israel. | | Zechariah | 3356 | 690 |
| Shallum reigns 1 month, and Menahem succeeds him (2 Kgs. 15:10-17) and reigns 10 years. | | Shallum Menahem | 3357 | 689 |
| Jotham is made ruler during the last years of Uzziah (2 Kgs. 15:5; 2 Chr. 26:21). | Jotham (as Judge) | | 3367 | 679 |
| Pekahiah reigns in 50th year of Uzziah (2 Kgs. 15:22-23). | | Pekahiah | 3368 | 678 |
| Pekah conspires against Pekahiah, slays him, and reigns in his stead (2 Kgs. 15:25-27). | | Pekah | 3370 | 676 |
| Isaiah's great vision (Isa. 6:1). Death of Uzziah. | | | 3371 | 675 |
| Jotham succeeds Uzziah in the 2nd year of Pekah (2 Kgs. 15:32-33). | Jotham (as king) | | 3371 | 675 |
| Ahaz succeeds Jotham in the 17th year of Pekah (2 Kgs. 15:38; 16:1-2). | Ahaz | | 3386 | 660 |
| Isaiah's prophecy, Ephraim to be broken in 65 years (Isa. 7:8). | | | 3387 | 659 |
| Hoshea slew Peka in the 20th year of Jotham, but was not made king until the 12th year of Ahaz (see explanation below) (2 Kgs. 15:30; 17:1). | | Interregnum | 3390 | 656 |
| Hoshea becomes king of Israel. | | Hoshea | 3398 | 648 |
| Hezekiah's accession as co-rex with Ahaz, 3rd year of Hoshea (2 Kgs. 16:20; 18:1-2). | Hezekiah | | 3401 | 645 |
| Death of Ahaz, Isaiah's prophecy against the Philistines (Isa. 14:28). | | | 3402 | 644 |
| Hezekiah as sole king. | | | 3403 | 643 |

| *Events* | *Judah* | *Israel* | *A.H.* | *B.C.* |
|---|---|---|---|---|
| Shalmaneser beseiges Samaria (2 Kgs. 18:9). | | | 3404 | 642 |
| Samaria taken. End of the kingdom of Israel (2 Kgs. 18:10). | | | 3406 | 640 |

The foregoing table covers a period of 174 years. It begins with a new dynasty in Israel, that of Jehu, who overthrew and completely exterminated the house of Omri, and stamped out Baal-worship. As a reward for this service, the Lord promised Jehu that his children of the fourth generation should sit upon the throne of Israel (2 Kgs. 10:30). We see, by the foregoing table, that this promise was fulfilled; for there were four kings of his line, Jehoahaz, Jehoash, Jeroboam II, and Zechariah.

But it is written that "Jehu took no heed to walk in the law of the LORD God of Israel with all his heart; for he departed not from the sins of Jeroboam which made Israel to sin" (2 Kgs. 10:31). Consequently, "In those days the LORD *began* to cut off the ends of Israel (marg.); and Hazael smote them in all the coasts of Israel, from Jordan eastward, all the land of Gilead, the Gadites and the Reubenites" (2 Kgs. 10:32-33).

This second period begins in Judah with a usurping queen, a daughter of the house of Ahab, on the throne, and with none left of the seed royal of the house of David but an infant of one year. Yet God did not suffer the house and lineage of David to be extinguished, but preserved the one frail life upon which it depended.

In the 7th year of Athaliah, Jehoiada the priest brought about a great political revolution, as a result of which the child Joash, then seven years of age, was proclaimed king, and Athaliah was put to death (2 Kgs. 11:1-16). At the same time Jehoiada brought about a great religious revival; for he caused the king and the people to enter into a covenant with the Lord, that they should be His people. Jehoiada, moreover, broke down the house of Baal, his altars and images, and slew Mattan, the priest of Baal (2 Kgs. 11:17-18). He also acted as instructor to the young king;

with the happy result that "Joash did that which was right in the sight of the LORD all his days wherein Jehoiada instructed him" (2 Kgs. 12:2). Jehoiada lived to be 130 years old, and was buried with royal honours among the kings in the city of David, "because he had done good in Israel, both toward God and toward his house" (2 Chr. 24:16).

But after the death of Jehoiada, Joash departed completely from the Lord. For he and all the princes of Judah left the house of the Lord, and served groves and idols; wherefore "wrath came upon Judah and Jerusalem for this their trespass" (2 Chr. 24:17-18). Moreover, when the Lord sent prophets to them to bring them again to Himself, they would not give ear; and when Zechariah the son of Jehoiada reproved them, they conspired against him, and stoned him with stones in the court of the house of the Lord. Wherefore the king of Syria came "and destroyed all the princes of the people from among the people. So they executed judgment against Joash. And when they were departed (for they left him in great diseases) his own servants conspired against him for the blood of the sons of Jehoiada the priest, and slew him upon his bed" (2 Chr. 24:19-25). Thus it is seen that the evil effects of Jehoshaphat's "affinity" with Ahab extended to the fourth generation.

Joash was succeeded by his son Amaziah, who also did well in the first part of his reign of 29 years, but towards the end he introduced the worship of the gods of the Edomites; wherefore God suffered him to be defeated by Jehoash, king of Israel, after which a conspiracy was made against him, and he was slain (2 Chr. 25).

## The Interregnum

From the statements of the text (2 Kgs. 14:17 and 2 Kgs. 15:1) it appears that the throne of Judah was vacant for a period of 11 years between the death of Amaziah and the accession of his son Uzziah (or Azariah, as he is called in Second Kings). This appears from the following facts: "Amaziah lived after the death of Jehoash, king of Israel, *fifteen years*" (2 Kgs. 14:17). This was

An. Hom. 3308 (see Table X). Uzziah did not come to the throne until the 27th year of Jeroboam II (2 Kgs. 15:1). The death of Jehoash was in the year 3293. Adding 27 years gives 3319 (by the Israelitish inclusive reckoning) as the year of Uzziah's accession. Thus we have, between 3308 and 3319, a period of 11 years, during which the throne of Judah was vacant. The reason why Uzziah was not crowned as king earlier is seen in the fact that, when he came to the throne, he was but 16, so that he was only 5 years old at the time of the death of his father, Amaziah.

There was also an interregnum in Israel between the reign of Jeroboam II and that of Zechariah; for Jeroboam's 41st year, which was his last, coincided with the 15th of Uzziah, king of Judah, and Zechariah did not succeed until the 38th of Uzziah (2 Kgs. 14:29; 15:8). This makes an interval of 22 years.

It was during the reign of Jeroboam II that Jonah the prophet, the son of Amittai, of Gath-hepher, prophesied (2 Kgs. 14:25). Those were days of "bitter" affliction in Israel (v. 26). It was the time of a great earthquake, the gravity of which is indicated by the fact that the prophet Amos, the herdsman of Tekoa, dated his prophecy with reference to its occurrence (Amos 1:1).

## The "Twentieth" Year of Jotham

In 2 Kgs. 15:30 is a statement which has given rise to what Anstey calls "one of the most interesting, and at the same time one of the most illuminating puzzles of the chronology of this period." The statement is that Hoshea made a conspiracy against Pekah, and slew him, and reigned in his stead, "in the *twentieth year of Jotham* the son of Uzziah." But Jotham reigned only *sixteen* years; so apparently we have, as Lightfoot said, "Jotham reigning four years after he is buried." But the statement is perfectly correct as a matter of chronology; for the death of Pekah did take place in the 20th year *after the accession* of Jotham. So the question is, why is the event dated from the beginning of Jotham's reign, instead of from that of Ahaz, who had been actually on the throne for four years? Why did the writer of 2 Kings ignore the accession of Ahaz? The reason is found in the extreme wickedness of King Ahaz, because of which "the LORD brought Judah low." For Ahaz "made Judah naked, and transgressed sore against the LORD." "He sacrificed to the gods of Damascus," which "were the ruin of him and of all Israel." And he "shut up the doors of the house of the LORD, and he made him altars in every corner of Jerusalem. And in every several city of Judah he made high places to burn incense unto other gods, and to provoke to anger the LORD God of his fathers" (2 Chr. 28:19-25). This explains why the accession of Ahaz is ignored in 2 Kgs. 15:30. As John Lightfoot says, "The Holy Ghost chooseth rather to reckon by holy Jotham in his grave than by wicked Ahaz alive."

## The Reign of Ahaz

King Ahaz, the father of Hezekiah, reigned for 16 years, and did wickedly from beginning to end:

> For he walked in the ways of the kings of Israel, and made molten images for Baalim. Moreover, he burnt incense in the valley of the son of Hinnom, and burnt his children in the fire, after the abominations of the heathen. Wherefore the LORD his God delivered him into the hand of the king of Syria; and they smote him, and carried away a great multitude of them captives, and brought them to Damascus. And he was also delivered into the hand of the king of Israel, who smote him with a great slaughter. For Pekah, the son of Remaliah, slew in Judah an hundred and twenty thousand in one day, all valiant men; because they had forsaken the LORD God of their fathers (2 Chr. 28:1-6).

Isaiah had prophesied during the hostilities between Judah and Rezin, king of Syria, and Pekah, king of Israel, declaring by the Word of the Lord that their attempt to take Jerusalem should not succeed. Isaiah also bore a message to Ahaz through the symbolical name of his son, *Shearjashub,* which means "the remnant shall return" (Isa. 7:1-8). Apparently the immediate fulfillment of this prophecy was the release, by Pekah's men (when met by the prophet Oded, by whom the Lord sent them a message) of the 200,000 captives (including women and children) which they had brought up with them out of Judah (2 Chr. 28:8-15).

## The Prophecy of the Virgin Birth of Christ

It was at this time that God, through Isaiah, sought to recover King Ahaz and to turn him to Himself and lead him to trust in Him, by bidding him ask a sign of the Lord, either in the depth or in the height above. But Ahaz was so hardened that he refused even to prove God in this way. This brought forth the prophecy of the Virgin-birth of Christ, which prophecy God addressed, not to Ahaz personally, but to "the house of David," of which Ahaz was the representative, saying: "Hear ye now, *O house of David;* Is it a small thing for you to weary men, but will ye weary my God also? Therefore, the LORD Himself shall give you a sign: Behold a virgin shall conceive and bear a son, and shall call his name Irnrmanuel" (Isa. 7:10-14). This is the first prophecy quoted in the New Testament (Mat. 1:20-23), and is, of course, of fundamental importance. It foretells the great event to which the chronological line of the Bible was leading – the coming of Christ. It further declares that the Son who was to be born to a virgin of the house of David, was God coming in the likeness of men, and for their salvation. But, what is most pertinent to our present purpose, it declares that, though the *men* of the house of David should be all as unfit to rule as was King Ahaz, nevertheless, God would raise up an horn of salvation in the house of His servant David, by causing *a virgin* to conceive and bring forth a Son, who should save His people from their sins.

It is recorded that, "At that time did king Ahaz send to the kings of Assyria for help.... For *the LORD brought Judah low because of Ahaz."* However, the king of Assyria "distressed him, but strengthened him not... And in the time of his distress did he trespass *yet more* against the LORD: *this is that king Ahaz"* (2 Chr. 28:16-22). So evil was the life of Ahaz that they buried him not in the sepulchres of the kings.

The period to which our attention is now directed (that which extends from the accession of Jehu as king of Israel to the extinction of the northern kingdom) is distinguished as the era of the prophets – Isaiah, Joel, Hosea, and others – through whom God, in His faithfulness, sent urgent and solemn warnings to His people, "rising up early and sending them," seeking thereby to turn the people from their evil ways, which were fast leading them to destruction, and to recall them to Himself. But the general trend of things was downward, and in the reign of King Ahaz conditions were at their worst. The recovery during the reign of Hezekiah was but for a time; and even the warning given by the judgment which overtook the kingdom of Israel did not avail to stem the tide of apostasy in Judah.

Had the people been living in obedience to the law there would have been no need to send prophets to them. Therefore the sending of the prophets was a mark of an evil state of the people. The general burden of all their messages was one of rebuke for the sins of the people, warnings of the consequences of persisting in their evil ways, and urgent calls to repent and return to the Lord.

# CHAPTER ELEVEN

## The Failure of Seven Prominent Kings of Judah

The kings of Israel were, without exception, depraved and ungodly men, wholly given over to idolatry and licentiousness. And it is a striking fact, worthy of our most thoughtful consideration, that their evil characters and deeds are stated in the Scriptures, without any attempt at concealment or palliation. Never were the annals of any kingdom so written by a *human* chronicler. Wherefore we have in this remarkable feature of Bible history a further proof of the Divine Authorship of the Holy Scriptures.

The history of the line of the kings of Judah is characterized by the same outspoken truthfulness, notwithstanding that there would be every incentive, humanly speaking, to glorify the house of David by concealing the faults and extolling the virtues of his descendants. Of some of the kings of Judah, it is stated in the baldest terms that they were wicked men; and of others, who did follow the Lord, their failures and departures are recorded quite as impartially as are their virtues.

Taking a rapid survey of the career of the most prominent kings of David's line, we may read therein some valuable lessons, and receive therefrom some wholesome and impressive warnings.

David, in his "last words" (2 Sam. 23:1-7), had declared by inspiration what God requires in those who rule over men, saying, "The God of Israel said, the Rock of Israel spake to me,

*He that ruleth over men must be just, ruling in the fear of God"*; and, being a prophet, David foresaw and foretold the failure of his own line, for he went on to say, *"Although my house be not so with God,* yet he hath made with me an everlasting covenant, ordered in all things and sure."

The subsequent history of David's line fully confirms this prophecy, making it quite clear that his house was "not so with God." Again and again we read of a king who began well, and continued for a longer or shorter time to walk "in the first ways of his father David," that is to say, in the fear of God, and according to the law of God, but who, later on, departed from those ways, some after one manner, some after another. It will be a profitable exercise to pass briefly in review the most prominent of those instances of departure from the right ways of the Lord.

1. Solomon, who was beloved of God, made a good start; and God blessed him with riches and honours in abundance, so that his kingdom is famed above all the kingdoms of the world for its glory and magnificence. For

> King Solomon exceeded all the kings of the earth for riches and for wisdom.... And the king made silver to be in Jerusalem as stones, and cedars made he to be as the sycamore trees that are in the vale for abundance.... And all king Solomon's drinking vessels were of gold, and all the vessels of the house of the forest of Lebanon were of pure gold; none were of silver, it was nothing accounted of in the days of Solomon (1 Kgs. 10:21, 23, 27).

But Solomon failed in the vital matter of *obedience to the law of the Lord.* Moses had expressly said, concerning the one who should be chosen for a king:

> But he shall not *multiply horses* to himself, nor cause the people to go down *to Egypt,* to the end that he should multiply horses.... Neither shall he *multiply wives* to himself, that *his heart turn not away;* neither shall he *greatly multiply to himself silver and gold. And it shall be,* when he sitteth upon the throne of his kingdom, that he shall write him a copy of this law in a

> book, out of that which is before the priests the Levites; and it shall be with him, and he shall read therein all the days of his life; that he may learn to fear the LORD his God, and to keep all the words of this law and these statutes to do them (Deut. 17:14-20).

Solomon violated the law in the most flagrant manner, in each of the three particulars expressly stipulated in the above Scripture. We have already quoted the passages which record how he *greatly* multiplied to himself silver and gold; and we further read that "Solomon loved many strange women, together with the daughter of Pharoah... And he had seven hundred wives, princesses, and three hundred concubines; and his wives *turned away his heart.* For it came to pass, when Solomon was old, that *his wives turned away his heart after other gods"* (1 Kgs. 11:1-8). Further it is written that "Solomon had forty thousand stalls of horses for his chariots, and twelve thousand horsemen" (1 Kgs. 4:26). "And Solomon gathered together chariots and horsemen; and he had a thousand and four hundred chariots, and twelve thousand horsemen, whom he bestowed in the cities for chariots, and with the king at Jerusalem. And a chariot came up, and went out of Egypt for six hundred shekels of silver, and an horse for an hundred and fifty" (1 Kgs. 10:26-29). Because of this flagrant disobedience, the Lord rent away the ten tribes from the kingdom of David.

2. King Asa also began well. He "did that which was right in the sight of the LORD, as did David his father. He took away the sodomites out of the land, and removed all the idols that his fathers had made" (1 Kgs. 15:11-15). Moreover, he "commanded Judah to seek the LORD God of their fathers, and to do the law and the commandment. Also he took away, out of all the cities of Judah, the high places and the images; and the kingdom was quiet before him" (2 Chr. 14:3-5). "And he brought into the house of God the things that his father had dedicated, and that he himself had dedicated, silver, and gold, and vessels" (2 Chr. 15:18). Thus Asa avoided the sin of multiplying gold and silver *unto himself,* and devoted those precious things to the Lord. Therefore, the

Lord greatly prospered him, and gave him rest on every side. Moreover, when the Ethiopians and the Lubims came against him with a huge host, and Asa cried to the Lord for help, He smote his enemies before him, insomuch that they were destroyed before the men of Judah; and they carried away very much spoil (2 Chr. 14:7-15). Nevertheless, afterwards, when Baasha came against Asa with a relatively small army, Asa *brought out* the silver and the gold out of the treasury of the Lord, in order to hire aid from the king of Syria, thus not only turning to man for help, but actually *bartering away the precious things of the Lord in order to procure it.* And not only so, but when God sent a prophet to reprove him, he flew into a rage, and put him in prison. And finally, when God chastened him by sending a disease upon him, Asa, in his sickness, sought not to the Lord, but to the physicians (2 Chr. 16:1-14). Thus in Asa we have the example of one who knew the Lord, and who "yet," in difficulty and sickness, *turned to man for help.*

3. Again in the history of King Jehoshaphat we find one who began well, and went on well for a time. We have already given a sufficiently full outline of the career of this good king. So we need only, for our present purpose, point out that Jehoshaphat's error was of a different character from that of his forefathers, Asa and Solomon. It consisted in "joining affinity" with Ahab, the utterly corrupt king of Israel, even going so far as to say to him, "I am as thou art, and my people as thy people, and we will be with thee in the war" (2 Chr. 18:1-3). That friendship with his ungodly neighbor caused far more damage to the house of David and to the people of Judah than the worst that Ahab could have inflicted by waging incessant warfare against them. Thus we learn from the career of Jehoshaphat the vital importance to the people of God of *separation from the world;* for "the friendship of the world is enmity against God" (Jas. 4:4). Jehoshaphat did not, like Solomon, multiply wives to himself, or horses, or silver and gold. Nor did he, like Asa, fail to seek the Lord in time of need (see 2 Chr. 18:4). But he became "unequally yoked together with unbelievers"; he had fellowship with unrigh-

teousness, and joined himself in a common cause with men of Belial (2 Cor. 6:14-17); and thereby he brought disaster upon himself and his posterity for four generations (Ex. 20:4).

4. Joash was a king who enjoyed from his infancy the great benefit of godly restraint and tuition under the care of Jehoiada, the priest. So it is recorded that "Joash did that which was right in the sight of the LORD all the days of Jehoiada the priest" (2 Chr. 24:2). But it appears that the commendable deeds of Joash were due to the strong influence of Jehoiada. There is no evidence that the heart of Joash was ever changed, but the contrary appears.

For, "after the death of Jehoiada came the princes of Judah, and made obeisance to the king. Then the king hearkened unto them; and they left the house of the LORD God of their fathers, and served groves and idols; and wrath came upon Judah and Jerusalem for this their trespass" (2 Chr. 24:17-18). Moreover, the people under Joash stoned the prophet whom God sent to reprove them; and Joash manifested the basest ingratitude toward the house of his benefactor, Jehoiada, by slaying his son. Therefore he was afflicted with "great diseases," and "his own servants conspired against him for the blood of the sons of Jehoiada the priest, and slew him on his bed, and he died; and they buried him in the city of David; but they buried him not in the sepulchres of the kings" (2 Chr. 24:20-25). From the career of Joash we may learn the immensely important fact that a good bringing up, and the restraints of good moral influences, though of very great value, are but external in their action, and do not avail for salvation and a new heart without personal faith and the *inward* work of "the washing of regeneration and renewing of the Holy Ghost" (Tit. 3:5). Without personal faith and the regenerating work of the Spirit of God it will surely happen "according to the true proverb, The dog is turned to his own vomit again, and the sow that was washed to her wallowing in the mire" (2 Pet. 2:22).

5. Amaziah, the son of Joash, was one who "did that which was right in the sight of the LORD, *but not with a perfect*

*heart"* (2 Chr. 25:2). He obeyed the voice of the prophet in dismissing the army of Israel which he had hired to help him; and God thereupon gave him victory over the Edomites. Yet, when he returned from the slaughter of the Edomites, he brought *their gods with him,* "and set them up to be his gods, and bowed down himself before them, and burned incense unto them. Wherefore the anger of the LORD was kindled against Amaziah, and he sent unto him a prophet which said unto him, Why hast thou sought after the gods of the people *which could not deliver their own people out of thine hand?"* (2 Chr. 25:6-15). Amaziah would not, however, receive this reproof, but silenced the messenger of God; and when he essayed to go to war against the king of Israel, he was defeated. The end of his career is told in these words: "Now after the time that Amaziah did turn away from following the LORD, they made a conspiracy against him in Jerusalem; and he fled to Lachish; but they sent to Lachish after him, and slew him there" (2 Chr. 25:27).

From the history of this king we may learn the inveterate disposition of the natural heart of man to turn to idols, and to trust in any creature rather than in the living God. The folly of trusting in the gods of a nation who could not deliver that nation is apparent. Yet such was the folly of this descendant of the wise King Solomon, and such were the gods chosen by this degenerate scion of the house of David.

6. Uzziah's reign was the next to the longest of all the kings, fifty-two years (Manassah reigned fifty-five). "And he did right in the sight of the LORD, according to all that Amaziah his father did. And he sought God in the days of Zechariah, who had knowledge of the visions of God, and as long as he sought the LORD, God made him to prosper" (2 Chr. 26:4-5). "But when he was strong, *his heart was lifted up to his destruction;* for he transgressed against the LORD, and went into the temple of the LORD to burn incense upon the altar of incense" (v. 16). This was the sin of *pride* and *presumption.* For Uzziah was not content with the honours of the throne, but desired those of the priesthood as well. But "no man taketh *this* honour to himself,

but he that is *called* of God as was Aaron" (Heb. 5:4). God had strictly separated the offices of king and priest. Only in Jesus Christ are they united. Hence, of all the characters in the Old Testament none was both a king and a priest, save Melchisedec, in whom the two offices were united only that he might stand as a type of Christ in His royal and eternal priesthood (Heb. 7:1-3). Therefore was Uzziah smitten with leprosy *for his presumption,* and had to live apart "in a several house" until the day of his death (2 Chr. 26:17-21). Hence Uzziah stands before us as a warning against the pride of the natural heart. Man is a sinner; and leprosy is a type of sin. He may effectually conceal the corruption of his heart from his fellow men; "but God looketh upon the heart"; and all things are naked and open unto the eyes of Him with whom we have to do. None can approach unto the presence of a holy God, except such as are "called," and are made fit for His presence by the Atonement which He has provided. When Uzziah transgressed this rule, which guards the sanctity of God's presence, the corruption that was in his heart was allowed *to come to the surface, where all could see it;* and then, in bitter humiliation, "he himself hasted to go out" (v. 21). If others could see what is in our hearts we would shun the light of day, and much more the light of God's holy Presence.

7. Finally, in Hezekiah we have doubtless the best of all the kings of David's line "after David himself; for it is written that "he did that which was right in the sight of the LORD according to *all* that David his father had done" (2 Chr. 29:2). "He trusted in the LORD God of Israel; so that after him was none like him among all the kings of Judah; nor any that were before him. For he clave to the LORD, and departed not from following him, but kept his commandments, which the LORD commanded Moses. And the LORD was with him, and he prospered whithersoever he went forth" (2 Kgs. 18:5-7). Of the chief incidents of his reign we shall speak later on. At this point we would only call attention to his conduct in the incident of the ambassadors from Babylon, who came to bring the congratulations of their king after that Hezekiah had been healed from a deadly sickness by the direct action

of God in answer to prayer. The incident is related three times (2 Kgs. 20:12-19; 2 Chr. 32:24-31; Isa. 39:1-8). In the account in 2 Chr. 32 it is stated that Hezekiah, after his miraculous recovery when sick unto death, "rendered not again according to the benefit done unto him; for *his heart was lifted up,* therefore there was wrath upon Judah and Jerusalem" (v. 25). His ingratitude and failure consisted in this, that when those heathen ambassadors of high rank and station came and paid their respects to him, he did not glorify the Lord, who had healed him, but, with puerile vanity, he displayed the baubles and showy trumpery, which constituted his own regal glory. For "he showed them all the house of *his* precious things, the silver and the gold, and the spices and the precious ointment, and all the house of his armour, and all that was found in his treasures; there was nothing in *his* house, nor in all his dominion that Hezekiah showed them not" (2 Kgs. 20:13). In all this there was not one word to the praise and glory of God. Wherefore, in 2 Chr. 32:31 we have this comment: "Howbeit, in the business of the ambassadors of the princes of Babylon, who sent unto him to inquire of the wonder that was done in the land, *God left him* to try him, that he might know all that was in his heart." Ingratitude and vanity were "in his heart," but he was unaware of it. Such sins, however, are very grievous in one on whom God has lavished the riches of His grace and mercy. Therefore God "left him," so that what was in the heart might come out, as in the case of Uzziah. How earnestly then ought we to pray continually, "lead us not into temptation"!

Here we have before us a complete sheaf of seven typical kings of Judah, illustrating the various ways in which one who "did run well" may falter, or stumble, or turn aside. We can make no better or more apt comment upon these inspired records, which have been written for our admonition, than that of the apostle Paul, who, speaking of the lessons which are to be found in the Old Testament types, said: "Wherefore, let him that thinketh he standeth take heed lest he fall" (1 Cor. 10:12).

In the case of all these kings it was prosperity and ease that led to their downfall. We may well, therefore, contrast with them the case of their father David, whose life was one of hardships, persecutions and afflictions, during the entire reign of Saul, and of conflicts and domestic troubles after he himself came to the throne. But in all that befell him he was humble, lowly minded, tender-hearted, submissive to the will of God, and always full of thanksgiving and praise to the Rock of his Salvation. Hence David made a *good ending;* for "he died in a good old age, full of days, riches and honour" (1 Chr. 29:28). Let such of us, therefore, as are advanced in years, seek grace continually that we may end well; and let our ambition be that of the apostle who said, "Neither count I my life dear unto myself, that I might *finish my course with joy*" (Acts 20:24).

# CHAPTER TWELVE

## The Kingdom of Judah From the Fall of Samaria to the Captivity

From the fall of Samaria, in the 6th year of Hezekiah, to the capture and destruction of Jerusalem by Nebuchadnezzar, in the 11th (and last) year of Zedekiah, was a period of 131 years. The following table shows the principal events of that period.

Table XI

| *Events* | *Kings of Judah* | *An. Hom.* | *B.C.* |
|---|---|---|---|
| Fall of Samaria in 6th year of Hezekiah (2 Kgs. 18:10). | Hezekiah | 3406 | 640 |
| In the 14th year of Hezekiah Judah was invaded by Assyrians under Sennacherib, fortified cities were taken (2 Kgs. 18:13); and Jerusalem besieged. But the Assyrian army was overthrown by the angel of the Lord (2 Kgs. 18:17-19:36). | | 3415 | 631 |
| In the same year occurred Hezekiah's illness and recovery; and also the visit of thc ambassadors of Merodach Baladan, king of Babylon (2 Kgs. 20:1-20). Sargon sent Tartan to Ashdod and took it (Isa. 20:1; 2 Kgs. | | | |

| *Events* | *Kings of Judah* | *An. Hom.* | *B.C.* |
|---|---|---|---|
| 18:17). All this was in the 14th year of Hezekiah. | | 3415 | 631 |
| God, in answer to prayer, added 15 years to the life of Hezekiah, who died and was succeeded by Manasseh (2 Kgs. 20:21) after reigning 29 years. | Manasseh | 3429 | 617 |
| Isaiah had prophesied (Isa. 7:8) in the days of Ahaz, that in 65 years Ephraim should be broken, that he should be no more a people. Sixty-five years from Ahaz's accession brings us to the days of Esar-haddon, and it is recorded in Ezra 4:2 that the "adversaries" had been transported into Palestine by Esar-haddon. Sixty-five years from Ahaz's first year would be | | 3452 | 594 |
| Manasseh reigned 55 years, and was succeeded by his son Amon (2 Kgs. 21:1, 18). | Amon | 3484 | 562 |
| Amon reigned 2 years, and was slain by servants who conspired against him, and succeeded by Josiah (2 Kgs. 21:23-26). | Josiah | 3486 | 560 |
| Josiah, in the 8th year of his reign, "while he was yet young" (16 years of age) "began to seek after the God of David, his father" (2 Chr. 34:3). | | 3494 | 552 |
| In the 12th year of his reign he began to purge Judah and Jerusalem by destroying the places of idol worship. | | 3498 | 548 |
| The prophet Jeremiah began to prophesy in the 13th year of | | | |

| *Events* | *Kings of Judah* | *An. Hom.* | *B.C.* |
|---|---|---|---|
| Josiah. He prophesied for 23 years to the 4th of Zedekiah (Jer. 1:2; 25:3). This establishes the chronology of that period. The beginning of Jeremiah's prophecy. | | 3499 | 547 |
| The purifying of Judah and Jerusalem (which occupied 6 years) completed. | | 3504 | 542 |
| In the same year (Josiah's 18th) the repairing of the Temple was begun, and the Book of the Law was found and read to Josiah, whose conscience was smitten upon hearing the words of the Law, because of the departures of the people therefrom. Josiah inquired of the Lord concerning this (2 Chr. 34:8-21). | | 3504 | 542 |
| In the same year (Josiah's 18th) was observed the great passover, concerning which it is recorded that "there was no passover like to that kept in Israel, from the days of Samuel, the prophet; neither did all the kings of Israel keep such a passover as Josiah kept" (2 Chr. 35:18-19). | | 3504 | 542 |
| Josiah, after reigning 31 years, was killed in battle with Pharoah Necho, king of Egypt, and was succeeded by his son Jehoahaz (2 Chr. 36:1), who reigned three months – | Jehoahaz | 3517 | 529 |
| Jehoahaz was carried captive into | | | |

| *Events* | *Kings of Judah* | *An. Hom.* | *B.C.* |
|---|---|---|---|
| Egypt, his brother Eliakim put on the throne by Pharoah Necho, and his name changed to Jehoiakim (2 Chr. 36:2-4). | Jehoiakim | 3517 | 529 |
| In Jehoiakim's 3rd year Nebuchadnezzar began to reign as co-rex (Dan. 1:1). This was the year of the captivity of Daniel and his three companions, the starting point of the 70 years' captivity foretold by Jeremiah (Jer. 25:11-12; Dan. 9:2). | | 3520 | 526 |
| Nebuchadnezzar began to reign as sole king in the 4th year of Jehoiakim (Jer. 25:1-3). That same year Jeremiah prophesied that all nations should serve the king of Babylon 70 years, after which he should be punished (Jer. 25:11-12). This establishes the date to the overthrow of Babylon by Darius and Cyrus. Other prophecies by Jeremiah that same year are found in Jer. 25:1-38; 27:6-7; 36:1-2; 45:1-5; 46:2. | | 3521 | 525 |
| In the 5th year of Jehoiakim (2nd of Nebuchadnezzar as sole king) Daniel interpreted Nebu-chadnezzar's dream of the Great Image of Gold, Silver, Brass, Iron and Clay. | | 3522 | 524 |
| Same year Jehoiakim rebelled against Nebuchadnezzar, after hav- | | | |

| *Events* | *Kings of Judah* | *An. Hom.* | *B.C.* |
|---|---|---|---|
| ing served him 3 years (2 Kgs. 24:1). | | 3522 | 524 |
| Same year Jehoiakim cut the Roll of the Book with a pen knife, and burned it in the fire (Jer. 36:22-23). | | 3522 | 524 |
| In the 7th year of Nebuchadnezzar he took captive 3023 Jews (Jer. 52:28). | | 3527 | 519 |
| In the 8th year of Nebuchadnezzar Jehoiakim died and was succeeded by Jehoiachin, who reigned only three months, when Nebuchnezzar besieged Jerusalem, took Jehoiachin to Babylon, with certain other captives, and treasures out of the Temple (2 Kgs. 24:8-16). He made Mattaniah (Jehoiachin's uncle) king in his stead, changing his name to Zedekiah (2 Kgs. 24:17). | Jehoiakim (Jeconiah-Coniah) | 3528 | 518 |
| | Zedekiah | 3528 | 518 |
| Ezekiel was carried away with Jehoiachin, and dates his prophecies from the captivity of Jehoiachin (see Ezek. 1:2; 40:1) year | | 3528 | 518 |
| Mordecai was also carried away in that captivity (Est. 2:5-6). | | 3528 | 518 |
| Ezekiel begins to prophecy in the 5th year of Jehoiachin's captivity (Ezek. 1:2). | | 3532 | 514 |
| In the same year (which was the 4th of Zedekiah), Hananiah uttered his false prophecy, and died under the hand of God (Jer. 28:1-17) | | 3532 | 514 |

| *Events* | *Kings of Judah* | *An. Hom.* | *B.C.* |
|---|---|---|---|
| Ezekiel's vision of the departure of the Glory of God from the Temple (Ezek. 8:1). | | 3533 | 513 |
| God refuses to be inquired of (Ezek. 20:1-3). | | 3534 | 512 |
| Nebuchanezzar beseiged Jerusalem in the 10th year of Zedekiah, 10th month, 9th day (2 Kgs. 25:1; Jer. 39:1; 52:4). | | 3537 | 509 |
| Jeremiah buys his uncle's field while Nebuchadnezzar was beseiging Jersusalem. Jeremiah imprisoned by Zedekiah (Jer. 32:1-13). | | 3538 | 508 |
| The end of Jeremiah's prophecies (Ezekiel's 40 years – Ezek. 4:5-6). | | 3538 | 508 |
| Ezekiel prophesies this same year against Tyre (26:1); against Pharoah (30:21); and against Egypt (31:1). | | 3538 | 508 |
| In the 11th year of Zedekiah famine prevailed in Jerusalem, city broken up (2 Kgs. 25:1-4; Jer. 39:2). Same year Nebuzaradan burnt Temple and broke down walls; Jerusalem carried away captive (Jer. 1:3). One comes to Ezekiel and tells him "the city is smitten" (Ezek. 33:21); Ezekiel's lamentation for Pharoah and Egypt (Ezek. 32:1, 17). | | 3539 | 507 |
| End of the kingdom of Judah, 11th year of Zedekiah (2 Kgs. 24:18). | | 3539 | 507 |

We will comment briefly upon some of the events of the period covered by the foregoing table:

The beginning of Hezekiah's reign was in bright contrast with that of his father Ahaz. For in the very first year of his reign he opened the doors of the house of the Lord, and charged the priests and Levites to sanctify themselves, and to cleanse the Temple. This was done in eight days; and thereupon Hezekiah gathered the rulers, went into the house of the Lord, and offered many offerings and sacrifices, besides setting the Levites to praise the Lord with the instruments of David, and the priests to praise with the trumpets (2 Chr. 29). Moreover, Hezekiah sent to all the remnant of Israel which had not been carried away into captivity; and he wrote letters to Ephraim and Manasseh, that they should come to the house of the Lord at Jerusalem to keep the passover unto the Lord God of Israel. But though "they laughed them [Hezekiah's messengers] to scorn and mocked them, nevertheless, divers of Asher, and Manasseh, and of Zebulun humbled themselves, and came to Jerusalem" (2 Chr. 30:1-11). Because of this, God had mercy upon Judah at that time, and spared them the fate that had overtaken the northern kingdom at the hands of the Assyrians in the 6th year of Hezekiah.

In this connection we should notice the message of Hosea, who also prophesied in the days of Uzziah, Jotham, Ahaz, and Hezekiah, kings of Judah, and of Jeroboam II, king of Israel. Hosea had three children, to each of whom had been given a prophetic name. The first was *Jezreel,* which means *the harvest of God,* signifying God's complete judgment upon the house of Jehu (Hos. 1:4, fulfilled 2 Kgs. 15:10). The second was *Lo-ruhamah,* meaning *I will not have mercy.* This signified that God would "no more have mercy on the house of Israel," but would "utterly take them away" (Hos. 1:6). "But," God said, "I will have mercy upon the house of Judah, and will save them *by the LORD their God, and will not save them by bow, nor by sword, nor by battle, by horses, nor by horsemen"* (Hos. 1:6-7).

This remarkable prophecy was fulfilled by the overthrow

of the hosts of Sennacherib, which had surrounded the walls of Jerusalem, and whose generals sent defiant and insulting messages to Hezekiah. The latter spread them before the Lord, and both the king and the prophet Isaiah "prayed and cried to heaven. And the LORD sent an angel, which cut off all the mighty men of valour, and the leaders and captains in the camp of the king of Assyria; so he returned with shame of face to his own land" (2 Chr. 32:1-21). This important incident is more fully described in Isaiah, chapters 36 and 37. There we have also God's answer to the prayer of Hezekiah, to whom God said: "For I will defend this city to save it for mine own sake, and for my servant David's sake. Then the angel of the LORD went forth, and smote in the camp of the Assyrians a hundred and fourscore and five thousand" (Isa. 37:35-36). This was in the 14th year of Hezekiah (Isa. 36:1). The destruction of Sennacherib's army by an angel, "a mighty one," had been foretold by Isaiah (Isa. 10:34).

The third child of Hosea was named *Lo Ammi*, meaning *not my people*: "For ye are not my people and I will not be your God" (Hos. 1:9). Likewise Isaiah prophesied: "Within three-score and five years shall Ephraim be broken that he be *not a people*" (Isa. 7:8).

In 2 Kgs. 25:21 is the record: "So Judah was carried away out of their land."

Also in the year of the fall of Samaria occurred Hezekiah's illness, when he was sick unto death, and God healed him in answer to prayer. This date is known because Hezekiah reigned 29 years (2 Chr. 29:1), and since God added 15 years to his life (2 Kgs. 20:6), it follows that the illness was in his 14th year. Then followed the unhappy incident of the Babylonian ambassadors, upon which we have already commented.

Manasseh, Hezekiah's son and successor, was born three years after his father's recovery, for he was twelve years of age when he began to reign (2 Kgs. 21:1).

## Sennacherib's Third Campaign

Among the tablets which have been recently exhumed in Assyria is a six-sided cylinder containing accounts of Sennacherib's military campaigns. In the light of Bible history it may be seen that these records are in the main authentic and correct, though written, of course, in such way as to reflect the greatest possible credit upon that proud monarch, and to heighten the lustre of his reign. The account of his third campaign is worth quoting for the purpose of comparison with the inspired narrative of the Bible:

> As for Hezekiah of Judah, who had not submitted to my yoke, 46 of his strong cities, together with innumerable fortresses and small towns dependent on them, by overthrowing the walls and open attack, by battle-engines and battering-rams, I besieged, I captured. I brought out from the midst of them and counted as spoil, 200,150 persons, great and small, male and female; besides mules, asses, camels, oxen, and sheep without number. *Hezekiah himself I shut up like a bird in a cage in Jerusalem, his royal city.* I built a line of forts against him, and kept his heel from going forth out of the great gate of his city. I cut off his cities which I had spoiled from the midst of his land, and gave them to Mentinti, king of Ashdod; Padi, king of Ekron; and Zil-baal, king of Gaza; and I made his country small. In addition to their former tribute and yearly gifts I added other tribute and the homage due to my majesty, and I laid it upon them. The fear of the greatness of my majesty overwhelmed him, even Hezekiah, and he sent after me to Nineveh, my royal city, by way of gift and tribute, the Arabs and his body guard whom he had brought for the defence of his royal city Jerusalem, and had furnished with pay, along with 30 talents of gold, 800 talents of pure silver, carbuncles, and other precious stones, a couch of ivory, thrones of ivory, an elephant's hide, an elephant's tusk, rare woods of all kinds, a vast treasure, as well as the eunuchs of his palace, and dancing men and dancing women, and he sent his ambassador to pay homage (or tribute) and to make submission.

It is true, as stated in 2 Kgs. 18:13-16, that Hezekiah did at first make submission to Sennacherib; for we read that he "appointed to Hezekiah, king of Judah, 300 talents of silver and 30 talents of gold; and Hezekiah gave him all the silver that was found in the house of the LORD, and in the treasures of the king's house. And at that time Hezekiah cut off the gold from the doors of the temple of the LORD, and from the pillars which Hezekiah, king of Judah, had overlaid, and gave it to the king of Assyria."

It is easy, however, to read between the lines of the inscription quoted above, that *Jerusalem was not taken.* But the inscription is significantly silent as to the reason why Sennacherib raised the siege of Jerusalem, and returned to his own land. The inscription makes very interesting reading in the light of 2 Chr. 32 and Isa. 36-37.

These Assyrian inscriptions are not dated.

## Manasseh and Amon

The reign of Manasseh, though the longest of all the kings (55 years, 3429-3484) calls for but little comment. He began to reign at the age of twelve years, "but did that which was evil in the sight of the LORD, like unto the abominations of the heathen." For he built up again the high places which Hezekiah had broken down; he caused his children to pass through the fire; he resorted to enchantments and witchcraft, and dealt with a familiar spirit and with wizards; and he set up a carved image which he had made in the house of God. And the Lord spoke to Manasseh and to his people, but they would not hearken (2 Chr. 33:10). Because of this, the Lord brought upon them the host of the Assyrians, who captured Manasseh, and carried him in chains to Babylon. When, however, he was in affliction he humbled himself greatly, and besought the Lord, who was entreated of him, and brought him again to Jerusalem. "Then Manasseh knew that the LORD he is God"; and thereafter he took away the idol out of the house of the Lord, and made other reformations (id. 11-19).

His son Amon reigned but two years (3484-3486), during which he did that which was evil in the sight of the Lord; and, moreover, he "humbled not himself before the LORD, as Manasseh his father had humbled himself; but Amon trespassed more and more" (2 Chr. 33:21-23). Wherefore his servants conspired against him, and slew him in his own house (v. 24).

## Reign of Josiah

It is recorded of Josiah that in the 8th year of his reign, "while he was yet young" (16 years), he began to seek after the Lord (2 Chr. 34:3), and he purged Judah and Jerusalem of idol worship. In the 18th year of his reign he repaired the house of the Lord. While this work was in progress Hilkiah the priest found a copy of the Book of the Law. Evidently, during the seventy-five years that had elapsed since the death of Hezekiah, the Word of God had been banished from the minds of king, priests, and people. When, however, Josiah heard the words of the Book, he greatly humbled himself, and sent to inquire of the Lord for them that were left of Israel and Judah. "For," said he, "great is the wrath of the LORD that is poured out upon us, because our fathers have not kept the word of the LORD, to do after all that is written in this book" (2 Chr. 34:1-21). The reply which came to him through Huldah the prophetess, whom his servants consulted, gave him to know that the Lord would surely bring upon that land, and upon the inhabitants thereof, all the curses written in the Book; but because Josiah's heart was tender, and he humbled himself when he heard the words of the Lord, the evil was deferred until after his days.

Moreover, Josiah went up to Bethel, where Jeroboam had founded the worship of the golden calf, and there fulfilled a prophecy which had been uttered about 350 years before by a man of God who had come out of Judah to cry against the altar, and who had said (1 Kgs. 13:1-3), "O altar, altar, thus saith the LORD; behold, a child shall be born unto the house of David, Josiah by name, and upon thee shall he offer the priests of the high places that burn incense upon thee, and men's bones shall be burnt upon thee." For the fulfillment see 2 Kgs. 23:15-18.

In the 18th year of his reign (3505) Josiah kept a most

solemn passover "according to the word of the LORD by the hand of Moses" (2 Chr. 35:6), concerning which it is recorded that "there was no passover like that kept in Israel, from the days of Samuel the prophet; neither did all the kings of Israel keep such a passover as Josiah kept, and the priests, and the Levites, and all Judah and Israel that were present, and the inhabitants of Jerusalem. In the eighteenth year of the reign of Josiah was this passover kept" (id. 18-19).

## Jehoahaz, Jehoiakim, Jehoichin, Zedekiah

No sooner was Josiah dead (3517) than the death-throes of the kingdom of Judah began. Jehoahaz (also called *Shallum),* who succeeded his father, reigned but three months, when he was deposed by Pharoah Necho, the king of Egypt, who placed his brother Eliakim on the throne, changing his name to Jehoiakim. And Necho carried Jehoahaz captive into Egypt.

Jehoiakim reigned 11 years. His evil character and deeds are set forth in the prophecy of Jeremiah. His attitude toward the word of God was rebellious and defiant, just the reverse of that of his father Josiah. This attitude was specially manifested in the incident recorded in Jer. 36:9-32, where it is related that, when Jehudi read to Jehoiakim the words of God by Jeremiah, which had been inscribed upon a roll, the king with his penknife cut the leaves as they were read, and cast them into the fire before which he was sitting in his winter house. This was in the fifth year of his reign (v. 9), the same year that Jehoiakim rebelled against Nebuchadnezzar, after having served him three years (2 Kgs. 24:1).

## Jeremiah's Prophecies

The prophecies of Jeremiah uttered during the reign of Jehoiakim are too long to be quoted here, or even described; but they should be read in connection with the study of this part of the chronology of the Bible. We will, however, refer briefly to the important prophecy in Jeremiah 22, where God speaks directly concerning the three kings, Jehoahaz, Jehoiakim, and Jehoiachin.

Concerning Shallum (Jehoahaz) he said:

> Weep ye not for the dead [Josiah, who had just died] but weep sore for him that goeth away [Jehoahaz]; for he shall return no more, nor see his native country. For thus saith the LORD touching Shallum, the son of Josiah, king of Judah, which reigned instead of Josiah his father; which went forth out of this place, he shall not return thither any more but he shall die in the place whither they have led him captive [Egypt] and shall see this land no more (Jer. 22:10-12).

By this we know that Jehoahaz died a captive in Egypt. His unrighteousness and covetousness are stated in verses 13-17, in contrast with the godliness of his father, Josiah.

Concerning Jehoiakim, the brother and successor of Jehoahaz, this word was spoken:

> Thereforth thus saith the LORD concerning Jehoiakim, the son of Josiah, king of Judah, They shall not lament for him, saying, Ah my brother! or Ah sister! they shall not lament for him saying, Ah lord! or, Ah his glory! He shall be buried with the burial of an ass, drawn and cast forth beyond the gates of Jerusalem (Jer. 22:18-19).

Concerning Jehoiachin (also called *Jeconiah,* and *Coniah)* this word was spoken:

> As I live, saith the LORD, though Coniah, the son of Jehoiakim, king of Judah, were the signet upon my right hand yet would I pluck thee hence. And I will give thee into the hand of them that seek thy life and into the hand of them whose face thou fearest, even into the hand of Nebuchadnezzar, king of Babylon, and into the hand of the Chaldeans. And I will cast thee out, and thy mother that bare thee into another country, where ye were not born; and there shall ye die. But to the land whereunto they desire to return, thither shall they not return. Is this man Coniah a despised broken idol? Is he a vessel wherein is no pleasure? Wherefore are they cast out, he and his seed, and are cast into a land which they know not? O earth, earth, earth [or *land, land, land*] hear the word of the LORD: Thus saith the LORD, Write

> this man childless, a man that shall not prosper in his days: for *no man of his seed shall prosper sitting upon the throne of David, and ruling any more in Judah* (Jer. 22:24-30).

This is a very notable prophecy. Jehoiachin was the last occupant of the throne of David in the direct line from father to son; for Mattaniah, whom Nebuchadnezzar placed upon the throne as his vassal, changing his name to Zedekiah, was Jehoiachin's *father's* brother (2 Kgs. 24:17); and *Zedekiah is not counted in the genealogy of Matthew 1.* Thus the line of David comes to an end, as a ruling line, with the solemn word and oath of the Lord that none of the last occupant's seed should sit upon the throne of David, or rule any more in Judah. But, in view of this it will be asked, what then becomes of God's oath which He swore to David, saying, "I have sworn unto David my servant, thy seed will I establish forever, and build up thy throne to all generations" (Psa. 89:3-4, 35-36)? And again: "The LORD hath sworn in truth unto David, he will not turn from it: of the fruit of thy body will I set upon thy throne" (Psa. 132:11)? And again, after Jehoiachin had been carried away to Babylon, the Lord said:

> David shall never want a man to sit upon the throne of the house of Israel; ...Thus saith the LORD, If ye can break my covenant of the day, and my covenant of the night, and that there should not be day and night in their season; then may also my covenant be broken with David my servant, that he should not have a son to reign upon his throne (Jer. 33:17-21).

It is a matter of the deepest interest to trace the complete fulfillment of both these lines of prophecy concerning David and his house, prophecies which seem on their face to contradict each other.

The genealogy of the royal line was carefully preserved and is given in Matthew 1, from Abraham and David (the two Old Testament pillars of the Gospel) to Joseph, the betrothed husband of Mary, of whom Christ was born. *This line runs through Jehoiachin (Jeconias),* but, according to the Word of God in Jer. 22:30, no man *of his seed* was to sit upon the throne of David or rule any more in Judah. This word, however, does not bar Jesus Christ, for He was not "of the seed" of Jeconiah, being born of a virgin, the Seed of the woman. But He was born *under the roof of Joseph, the son of Jeconiah, the heir to the throne,* and of one whom Joseph had betrothed to himself as his wife. Hence, under the law of Israel, He was entitled to the throne.

The other prophecy, which pledged the throne to David's seed forever, is also fulfilled in that Mary, the mother of Jesus Christ, was of the house of David, *but her descent* (given in Luke 3) *does not come through Jeconiah* and the other kings of Judah, but through David's son Nathan, the younger brother of Solomon, Nathan being also a son of Bathsheba (1 Chr. 3:5).

God's stern word concerning Coniah, that though he were a signet upon His hand, yet would He pluck him thence (Jer. 22:24) should be compared with His gracious word to Coniah's grandson, Zerubbabel (for the relationship see Mat. 1:12) who rebuilt the Temple, and to whom God said, "In that day will I take thee, O Zerubbabel, the son of Shealtiel, saith the LORD, and *shall make thee as a signet,* for I have chosen thee, saith the LORD" (Hag. 2:23).

## Zedekiah's Reign

Many important events occurred in the eleven years of Zedekiah; but these are set forth with sufficient fulness for our purposes in the table; so we will not comment further upon them. We will refer only to a single prophecy (that in Ezekiel 21) which is of exceptional importance, for it pronounced the doom of Israel at the hands of Nebuchadnezzar, and the downfall of Zedekiah. In it are these words:

> I have set the point of the sword against all their gates, that their heart may faint and their ruins be multiplied. Ah! it is made bright, it is sharpened [marg.] for the slaughter. And thou, profane wicked prince of Israel [Zedekiah], whose day is come, when iniquity shall have an end, Thus saith the LORD God, Re-

> move the diadem, and take off the crown; this shall not be the same. Exalt him that is low, and abase him that is high. *I will overturn, overturn, overturn it; and it shall be no more, until he come whose right it is; and I will give it him.*

Thus it was decreed that the crown should be taken away, and the throne of David overturned, and that none of his line should wear the crown until Jesus Christ, of the seed of David, should be raised from the dead and crowned in heaven, the King of the Kingdom of heaven, "the king eternal, immortal, invisible, the only wise God, to whom be honour and glory forever and ever. Amen" (1 Tim. 1:17).

The Eighty-ninth Psalm is a prophecy concerning David and his house. It might appropriately be entitled, "The Sure Mercies of David," for it contains a sevenfold promise of the perpetuity of God's "mercy" to that chosen one.

But, beginning at verse 30, God plainly says: "If his children forsake my law, and walk not in my judgments; if they break my statutes, and keep not my commandments; then will I visit their transgression with the rod, and their iniquity with stripes." This was fulfilled again and again in the experiences of David's successors. But a still more severe visitation was needed; and in verses 38 to 47 of the Psalm we find a wonderful foretelling of the long period (over five hundred years) during which the house of David was brought low. With bitter grief the prophet says: "But thou hast cast off, and abhorred, thou hast been wroth with thine anointed. Thou hast made void the covenant of thy servant.... Thou hast made his glory to cease and *cast his throne down to the ground.*"

Nevertheless, God never forgot that He had made with David "an everlasting covenant, ordered in all things and sure" (2 Sam. 23:5).

# CHAPTER THIRTEEN

## The Captivity and the Return "Unto the Messiah"

The true beginning of the captivity was in the year 3520, when Daniel and others were taken captive to Babylon, in third year of Jehoiakim (Dan. 1:1). Anstey dates the seventy years of Jer. 25:11-12 and Dan. 9:2, from this date (see Table XI). From this date onward we have to do with two periods of time whereof the measures are given to us *prophetically,* rather than *historically.* The first is a period of *seventy years,* announced in Jer. 25:11-12 and mentioned in Dan. 9:2, and the other is a period of seventy *sevens* of years, announced by the angel Gabriel in Dan. 9:24-27. The longer period begins where the shorter period ends, that is, with the notable decree of Cyrus (Ezra 1:1-4), which brought to an end the captivity of the Jews, and which started again their national existence. The seventy sevens ("weeks") of years is the measure "determined" by God in advance (Dan. 9:24), of that second period of Jewish history, which extended from the decree of Cyrus in the first year of his reign, to and including the crucifixion and resurrection of "the Messiah."

In our last table (XI) we gave the chronology to the end of the reign of Zedekiah, in order to complete the history of the kings of Judah. So we begin our next and final table at that point.

Table XII

| *Events* | *An. Hom.* | *B.C.* |
|---|---|---|
| Zedekiah carried into captivity. . . . . . . . . . . . . . . | 3539 | 507 |
| Ezekiel's vision of the new land, city, and temple (14th year after the city was smitten) see Ezek. 40:1 . . . . . . . . . . . . . . . . . . . . . . . | 3552 | 494 |
| Evil Merodach, king of Babylon (successor to Nebuchanezzar) brought Jehoiachin out of prison, and set his throne above the thrones of the kings that were with him in Babylon (2 Kgs. 25:27; Jer. 52:31) . . . . | 3564 | 482 |
| In the 1st year of Belshazzar (who succeeded Evil Merodach) Daniel's vision of the Four Beasts was given (Dan. 7:1) . . . . . . . . . . | 3584 | 462 |
| In the 3rd year of Belshazzar the vision of the Ram and He-goat was given to Daniel (Dan. 8:1) . . . . . . . . . . . . . . . . . . . . . . | 3586 | 460 |
| The kingdom was taken by Darius the Mede, and the city of Babylon was taken by Cyrus (Dan. 5:26-31), as foretold by Isaiah (Isa. 45:1-4). Darius and Cyrus rule jointly. The vision of the Seventy Weeks given to Daniel (Dan. 9:1) . . . . . . . . . . . . . . . . . . | 3587 | 459 |
| Cyrus becomes sole king. Issues proclamation in his 1st year releasing the captive Jews and giving permission to "go up and build the house" (Ezra 1:1-4). *This year marks the end of the 70 years' captivity, and the beginning of the 70 sevens of years "determined" upon Daniel's people and his holy city, to finish the transgression,* etc. (Dan. 9:24) . . . . . . . . . . . . . . . . . . . . . | 3589 | 457 |
| In the 7th month of the year last mentioned (the 1st of Cyrus, An. Hom. 3589) the people gathered themselves together as one man to Jerusalem. But not until the "second year of their coming to the house of God at Jerusalem, in the second month" did they | | |

| *Events* | *An. Hom.* | *B.C.* |
|---|---|---|
| begin "to set forward the work of the house of the LORD" (Ezra 3:1-8). (The intervening seven months would doubtless have been needed for building habitations for themselves). So we have the date of the beginning of the second Temple . . . . . . . . | 3590 | 456 |
| In the 3rd year of Cyrus (Dan. 10:1) Daniel had the vision recorded in Chaps. 10-12 of his prophecy, in course of which he was informed that three kings of Persia should yet stand up (after Cyrus) and that the fourth should be far richer than they all (Dan. 11:2). This 4th king was the fabulously wealthy monarch Xerxes, who "stirred up all against the realm of Grecia"; and the "mighty king" who succeeded him, and whose kingdom was broken, and divided toward the four winds of heaven, but not to his posterity, was Alexander the Great, whose kingdom was divided between his four generals. This vision was in the year (the 3rd of Cyrus) . . | 3591 | 455 |
| From the decree of Cyrus in his 1st year there were to be "seven weeks and three-score and two weeks unto the Messiah, the Prince" (Dan. 9:25). The "seven weeks" (49 years) are apparently the measure of the "troublous times" during which the street and wall of the city were to be built. This would bring us (reckoning being inclusive of the year the decree was issued) to the year . . . . . . . . . . . . . . . . . . . . . . . . . . . | 3637 | 409 |
| From the 1st year of Cyrus "unto Christ," that is (as will be shown below), to His baptism, was 483 years, which would bring us to the year 4071; and since the Lord was then beginning to be 30 years of age, we have for the year of His birth (4071–30=) . . . . | 4041 | A.D. 5 |

| *Events* | *An. Hom.* | *A.D.* |
|---|---|---|
| Add 30 years to His baptism (15th year of Tiberius Cæsar) = . . . . . . . . . . . . . . . . . . . . . . . . | 4071 | 26 |
| Add 3½ years to His Crucifixion, Resurrection and Ascension, and the coming of the Holy Spirit, and we have, as the year of those, the greatest by far of all events in the history of the heavens and the earth . . . . . | 4075 | 30 |

The determination of the Crucifixion as having occurred in the year 30 A.D. is according to Clinton, and nearly all modern chronologers, who assign 3½ years to His ministry, on the basis of what appears in the Gospel of John.

As to this John Lightfoot says:

> Of all the four Evangelists John is most punctual. Nay, he only is punctual to give account of the festivals that intercurred between Christ's entrance into His public ministry at His baptism, and the time of His death, *that renowned and signal space of time of half a week of years,* as they be called in Daniel 9:27, or *three years and a half,* in which Christ performed His ministry and wrought Redemption.

## The End and Aim of the Chronology

Here ends the chronology of the Bible. The Messiah came in "the fullness of the time." He came to His own, and His own received Him not. They rejected Him, betrayed Him, and with wicked hands (the hands of Gentiles) crucified and slew Him. "But God raised Him from the dead." *With His Resurrection began the New Creation.*

The count of the years of the history of Adam, the man by whom sin entered into the world, and death by sin, is ended. For the line of sacred chronology has conducted us to the Man who came, in the end of the age, to put away sin by the sacrifice of Himself, who has brought life and immortality to light, and whose Kingdom has no chronology, because it is "without end."

John Lightfoot makes this luminous comment upon the chronology of the Bible, showing why it goes so far (and with such painstaking care) and *no farther:*

> The Holy Ghost draws up a chronicle of times from the Creation to the Redemption; from the *beginning* of time to the *fullness* of it, namely from the beginning of the world to the death and resurrection of Christ, and to that which resulted from it, Pentecost, fifty days after. The reason whereof is because, by links and links of time, God would draw men on to observe how He was numbering and counting out the years towards *that great time of promise and expectation,* and to observe also *(when that great matter was accomplished) how faithful God had been through all changes and vicissitudes of times to carry on that great promise.* Accordingly it pleased God, in the era before that great work of Redemption, to certify His people oft when they fell into misery, nay oft even *before* they fell into it, how long the time of their affliction and oppression should be, in order that still they might be carried on to look for deliverance, and that by the deliverance they might still have an eye to the promise, and be confirmed in the promise concerning deliverance by Christ.

But now that the great work of Redemption is accomplished, and there is salvation full and free for all men, there is no occasion for the counting of the years to a great coming event. The Redeemer has entered into His rest and His glory, having by Himself purged our sins; and what His people *now* have to sustain them while on earth is, not a promise of deliverance at a specified time, but grace to sustain them during *all* trials, with the command to be always watching for His coming again, since they know not in what hour their Lord may come (Mat. 24:42). Now that eternal redemption has been accomplished, there is no need for counting the years and giving measures and links of time. The dispensation of grace has no "times and seasons."

## The Christian Era

The Christian Era should properly begin with the year

Christ was born; and in devising it, the intention was to have it begin with that year. By the "Christian Era" is meant the system upon which calendars are constructed, and by which historical events are now dated in practically all the civilized world. But the originator of the system made a miscalculation as to the year (in the calendar then in use) in which Christ was born, as the result of which the year A.D. 1 was fixed *four years too late.* In other words, the Lord Jesus was four years old in the year A.D. 1.

The mistake came about in this way: The Christian Era (i.e. the scheme of dates beginning A.D. 1) was not devised until A.D. 532. Its inventor, or contriver, was a monk named Dionysius Exiguus. At that time the system of dates in common use began from the era of the emperor Diocletian, A.D. 284. Exiguus was not willing to connect his system of dates with the name of that infamous tyrant and persecutor. So he conceived the idea of connecting his system with, and dating all its events from, *the Incarnation of Jesus Christ.* His reason for wishing to do this was, as he wrote to Bishop Petronius, "to the end that the commencement of our hope might be better known to us, and that the cause of man's restoration, namely, our Redeemer's passion, might appear with clearer evidence."

For the carrying out of this excellent plan, it was necessary to fix the date of the Incarnation in the terms of the chronological systems then in vogue. The Romans dated the beginning of their history from the supposed date of the founding of the city *(ab urbe condita* or A. U. C as usually abbreviated). Dionysius Exiguus calculated that the year of our Lord's birth was A. U. C. 753. He made his equivalence of dates from Luke 3:1, "Now in the *fifteenth year* of the reign of Tiberius Caesar" etc., at which time Christ was 30 years of age according to Luke 3:23. But it was ascertained later that a mistake of four years had been made; for it clearly appears by Matthew 2 that Christ was born *before the death of Herod,* who died in 749 A.U.C. Tiberius succeeded Augustus, Aug. 19, A.U.C. 767. Hence his 15th year would be A.U.C. 779; and from those facts Dionysius was right in his calculation. But it was discovered in later years that Tiberius began to reign as colleague with Augustus four years before the latter died. Hence the 15th year mentioned by Luke was four years earlier than was supposed by Dionysius, and consequently the birth of Christ was that many years earlier than the date selected by Exiguus, which date has been followed ever since. This must be allowed for in any computation of dates which involves events happening before Christ.

We have now found, according to our reckoning, that Christ was born An. Hom. 4041. Therefore, His crucifixion, when He was in His 34th year, would be 4041+34=4075. This is equivalent to 30 A. D.; and to get the true measure of years of any event in our era from the Incarnation it is necessary to add four years to its accepted date.

To get the corresponding date in terms of B. C. for any event of Old Testament history, it is only necessary to deduct the years An. Hom. from 4046. For the birth of Christ being 4041 An. Hom. and the Christian era four years later, then B. C. 1 would be equivalent to 4045 which is 4046–1.

We have given the B.C. dates in our tables, in a parallel column alongside of the corresponding An. Hom. dates.

# CHAPTER FOURTEEN

## The "Seventy Weeks" of Daniel - When Do They Begin and End?

Some questions of deep interest arise in connection with the period covered by our last chronological table; but they are questions of interpretation of Scripture, rather than questions of chronology. All expositors are agreed (so far as we are aware) that the message brought by Gabriel to Daniel gives the measure *of years,* from the going forth of the commandment to restore and to build Jerusalem, unto the Messiah, the Prince, as *sixty-nine sevens of years,* that is, 483 years. But there is much difference of opinion as to, *first,* what decree it was from which the time began to run, and *second,* what event it was in the lifetime of our Lord to which the 483 years brings us. It is manifest that, unless those two points (the beginning and the ending of the 483 years) can be established with certainty, we cannot continue our chronology down to the Cross and Resurrection of Christ, and the consequences would be that the dated line, so carefully preserved for 3500 years, would fail to reach its objective. But, after much study of the entire subject, we are convinced that the Scriptures do not leave us in uncertainty as to those essential matters of fact. Indeed, it will be seen by what follows that, on the contrary, both events are marked and dated with unusual exactitude. Furthermore, it has become quite clear to us that the differences of opinion, to which we have referred, have arisen altogether from the fact that some of our able and painstaking chronologers and expositors have adopted the mistaken estimates of Ptolemy as the foundation of their systems of dates, instead of grounding themselves upon the chronology of the Bible itself. Having committed themselves to a chronological scheme which makes the era of the Persian Empire about 80 years too long, they have been compelled to construe the statements of Scripture in such wise as to force them into agreement with that scheme; and inasmuch as the measure of 483 years from the first year of Cyrus would, if Ptolemy's table be accepted, come short, by many years, of any event in the lifetime of Christ, one must either abandon that table, or else must search for a decree of a Persian king, many years nearer to Christ, to serve as the starting point of the Seventy Weeks of Daniel. The trouble, therefore, is not that there is any uncertainty in the Scriptures, but that expositors have turned aside from the Scriptures, and have accepted, for the 500 years immediately preceding the coming of Christ, a defective chronology based upon heathen traditions.

In another place we have discussed at considerable length[1] the many interesting questions that have arisen concerning the prophecy of the Seventy Weeks, so we shall not go extensively into that subject here. It is appropriate, however, that the main reasons for the conclusions we have reached should be set forth with sufficient fulness to enable the readers of this book to examine them in the light of Scripture.

Our main conclusions are:

*First,* that the canon of Ptolemy is untrustworthy as a basis for a system of chronology, its statements being not authenticated in any way; and that, therefore, it should be rejected as unworthy of our confidence, even if it did not come into conflict with the statements of Scripture;

*Second,* that "the commandment to restore and to build

---

1. See *The Seventy Weeks and the Great Tribulation* (S. E. Roberts Publishers).

Jerusalem," from which the prophetic period of Seventy Weeks began to run (Dan. 9:25), was the decree of Cyrus the Great, referred to in Ezra 1:1-4;

*Third,* that the 483-year period of Dan. 9:25, reaching "unto the Messiah, the Prince," ended at *the baptism of our Lord,* in the 15th year of Tiberius Caesar, when He was thirty years of age.

## I. The Canon of Ptolemy

In Chapter Two of this book we have pointed out that Ptolemy was not a contemporary historian of the events of the Persian Empire, whose chronology he attempts to set forth, but flourished *more than six centuries* after that Empire began. Therefore he cannot be accepted as an authority for the events of that period. Nor does he claim that he had access to any records contemporary with those events. We have also pointed out that, not only are the chronological statements of Ptolemy entirely uncorroborated, but they are contradicted by authorities which are more entitled to confidence than he. Thus, whereas Ptolemy estimates that there were *ten* Persian kings in all, Josephus, an earlier writer and one who has a stronger claim upon our confidence, gives only *six.* Moreover, this agrees much better with the statement of the angel to Daniel, in the 3rd year of Cyrus, that there were yet *four* kings of Persia to stand up, the fourth being plainly identified as the great and wealthy Xerxes, whose expedition against "the realm of Grecia" ended, as is known from secular history, so disastrously. Those who accept the canon of Ptolemy must believe there were *eight* kings between Cyrus and Xerxes, the last of the Persian kings, and must accept the length of years which Ptolemy assigns to their respective reigns, and which he figures out to be a total of *205 years*. In contrast with Ptolemy's estimates, the Jewish and Persian traditions make the period of the Persian Empire a period of *52 years* (Anstey, p. 232). We do not accept the estimates of Josephus any more than those of Ptolemy, and have no need of either; but the statements of the former do serve to show that those of the latter are not to be relied upon.

Further Anstey says:

> There are no contemporary chronological records whatever to fix the dates of any of the Persian monarchs after Darius Hystaspes. The clay tablets of Babylon fix the chronology, for the reigns of Cyrus, Cambyses, Pseudo-Smerdis, and Darius Hystaspes; but they do not determine the date of any subsequent Persian king. The dates which have reached us, and which are now generally received as historical, are a late compilation made in the 2nd century A.D. and found in Ptolemy's canon. They rest upon the calculations or guesses made by Eratosthenes, and certain vague, floating traditions, in accordance with which the period of the Persian empire was mapped out as a period of 205 years.

## The Futility of Eclipses and Other Astronomical Phenomena as Aids to Chronology

The attempt to supply missing links in the chain of chronology by means of eclipses, and astronomical calculations, is utterly futile. It is a simple matter, indeed, for astronomers to make a perfect chart of all solar and lunar eclipses, and to fix the time of their several occurrences with great exactitude. But that does not help matters in the least; for the trouble is that, when a historical fragment is found which contains a reference to an eclipse, it is impossible to tell which of the charted eclipses, within say a century, is the one referred to. And even could that be done it would serve only to fix the date of *one* event.

It must be remembered that chronology is not merely or chiefly a matter of intervals of time. It is primarily a matter of *historical events,* their sequence, and the number of years *from one known event to another.* Astronomers can indeed give us the precise order and dates of all eclipses which occurred between the days of Cyrus and those of Alexander the Great, or of any other period. But eclipses are events which occur in the heavens, whereas chronology has to do with happenings on earth. Astronomers cannot tell us the succession of the Persian kings, or the length of their several reigns. That information is what is needed to make a chronology, and without it, a perfect chart of all the eclipses is of no more value for the purpose than a map of the moon.

Therefore, as regards the events of sacred history prior to the conquest of Asia by Alexander the Great, there are *no sources of information, apart from the Bible itself,* whereby the chronology thereof can be established. But none are needed, because the chronology of the Bible is complete in itself. Manifestly, it was no more a part of God's plan of revelation that we should be dependent upon human sources for the completion of sacred chronology, than that we should be dependent upon such sources for the completion of any part of essential truth or doctrine.

## II. The Commandment to Restore and to Build Jerusalem (Dan. 9:25)

The going forth of the commandment (lit. *word)* to restore and to build Jerusalem is one of the most important of the chronological landmarks of Scripture; for from it stretches the measuring line of 483 years "unto the Messiah, the Prince." This is a matter that Daniel was specially charged by the angel to "know" and to "understand." Unless the time of the going forth of that word be *known,* and unless its relation with the entire chronological scheme of the Bible be *understood,* the divinely-given measuring line will be of no avail for the very purpose for which it was given. We believe, however, and will seek now to show, that the Scriptures give, and with a clearness which leaves nothing to be desired, both the decree referred to, and also *the date* of its "going forth." Indeed it is not likely there would ever have been a question about it, were it not that some able and learned men have gone to the Bible with a ready-made chronology, based on the miscalculations of Ptolemy, and have sought to make the statements of Scripture agree thereto, instead of pursuing the true method, namely, finding *in the Bible* the monumental events which mark respectively the beginning and the end of the prophetic period, and then permitting the Scripture itself to tell them the number of years (483) between those terminal events.

Let it be noted that the time specified by the angel was to begin, not at the restoring and building of the city, but at the *going forth* of the "word," or decree, to restore and to build. That "word" *went forth* in the first year of Cyrus, king of Persia, and, moreover, its going forth was for the express purpose "that the word of the LORD by the mouth of Jeremiah might be fulfilled" (Ezra 1:1). To that end the Lord Himself "stirred up the spirit of Cyrus, king of Persia, that he *made a proclamation* [lit, *caused a voice to pass,* see marg.] *throughout all his kingdom."* Here certainly was a royal "word" or proclamation *going forth.* And the express object of it was to release the captives of Judah that they might "go up *to Jerusalem,* which is in Judah, and build the house of the LORD God of Israel (he is the God), which is in Jerusalem" (Ezra 1:2-3).

The immediate effect of the going forth of this word was that a large number of Israelites (42,370 besides 7,337 servants and maids) "went up out of the captivity... and came again *unto Jerusalem* and Judah" (Ezra 2:1, 64-65); and other companies came later. This was precisely what Daniel was praying for and looking for. It was the ending of the captivity of his people, and the beginning of a new term of existence for the nation and the city. He had prayed: "O my God, incline thine ear, and hear; open thine eyes and behold our desolations, *and the city which is called by thy name;* ...defer not for thine own sake, O my God; for *thy city and thy people are called* by thy name" (Dan. 9:19).

To "restore" means, in all occurrences of the Old Testament word, to "turn back," and hence to replace what had been taken away. In this case it plainly meant to restore the people to the city, and thus re-constitute the latter. That such was the purport, and also the immediate effect, of the decree of Cyrus is left in no doubt whatever; for it is written that the captives released by the decree of Cyrus "came again unto Jerusalem and Judah, every one *unto his city"* (Ezra 2:1); and again that they "dwelt *in their cities,* and all Israel *in their cities"* (2:70). This includes, of course, and pre-eminently, the chief city, Jerusalem.

## Isaiah's Prophecy Concerning Cyrus

In the Book of Ezra the matter, concerning which we are inquiring, is stated *historically,* and with all necessary clearness. But, to put it beyond all doubt, and to show, moreover, how surpassingly important was this official action of King Cyrus in the eyes and in the purposes of God, we call attention to the remarkable fact that God had also declared it *prophetically* by His prophet Isaiah, more than 150 years previously, even calling by name the king who was to fulfill His pleasure. For Isaiah had prophesied concerning Cyrus, saying, "Thus saith the LORD... that confirmeth the word of his servant, and performeth the counsel of his messengers; that *saith to Jerusalem, Thou shalt be inhabited;* and to the cities of Judah, Ye shall be built, and I will raise up the decayed places thereof,... *that saith of Cyrus,* He is my *shepherd, and shall perform all my pleasure; even saying to Jerusalem, Thou shalt be built; and to the temple, Thy foundation shall be laid"* (Isa. 44:24-28).

Thus we have God's own word for it that Cyrus, and none other, was to speak the "word" to restore and to build Jerusalem, even *"saying,* Thou shalt be built."

Furthermore, Cyrus was made aware of this prophecy of Isaiah, doubtless by Daniel; for in his decree he said, "The God of heaven *hath charged* me to build him an house at Jerusalem" (Ezra 1:2); and it will be observed that the same "charge" included both the building of the Temple, and the building of *the city* (Isa. 44:28).

Furthermore, in the next chapter (Isa. 45:13) God speaks of Cyrus, saying, *"He shall build my city, and he shall let go my captives,* not for price nor reward, saith the LORD of hosts." Here the letting go, or *restoring,* of the captives is coupled with *the building of the city.*

We are taking pains to point out fully the proof that it was from Cyrus that the word to restore and to build the city went forth, because those who wish to make the statements of Scripture conform to the mistaken chronology of Ptolemy point to the fact that the building of the *city* is not expressly spoken of in Ezra 1:1-4. Ezra does not indeed quote the entire decree, and the city is not specifically mentioned in the part quoted. But he does make perfectly clear that this was the "word to restore and to build Jerusalem"; for Jerusalem was the objective point of the decree; its former inhabitants were permitted, and even *commanded,* to return to it, and they *did* return to it; and that command, coupled with the command to "build the house of the LORD," would necessarily involve building habitations for the inhabitants of the city.

## The Building of the City

Furthermore it is recorded that in the 7th month (of the 1st year of Cyrus), "the people gathered themselves together as one man *to Jerusalem"* (Ezra 2:1). Of course their first necessity would be to erect houses for themselves; and this would explain why it was not until "the second year of their coming to the house of God at Jerusalem, in the second month" that Zerubbabel and Jeshua, and "all they that were come out of the captivity into Jerusalem" began "to set forward the work of the house of the LORD" (Ezra 3:8). That interval of seven months would be needed to build houses for the people, and defenses for the city.

From that time onward, in the historical books of Ezra and Nehemiah, and in the prophecy of Zechariah, Jerusalem is spoken of as an *existing city.* The Temple was finished "in the sixth year of the reign of Darius the king" (Ezra 6:15); and the children of Israel which were come again out of the captivity kept the feast of unleavened bread seven days (Ezra 6:21-22). This implies that the city was capable of accommodating great numbers of people.

In chapters 7 and 8 of Ezra, we read of the coming of Ezra himself, with a company of people, including women and children, *to Jerusalem* (8:32).

In chapter 9 Ezra prays to God, and extols His goodness in giving them favour in the sight of the kings of Persia "to set up the house of our God, and to repair the desolations thereof, and *to give us a wall* in Judah and *in Jerusalem"* (Ezra 9:9).

In chapter 10 it is recorded that Ezra and the leaders "made proclamation throughout Judah *and Jerusalem* unto all the children of the captivity, that they should gather themselves together *unto Jerusalem"* (v. 7), which they did. Yet there be some who would ask us to believe that not only was there no rebuilding of the city up to that time, but that the *word* for the restoring and building thereof did not go forth until the 20th year of Artaxerxes, referred to in the second chapter of Nehemiah.

## Nehemiah's Work

Some who accept as correct the chronology of Ptolemy, based upon the guesses of Eratosthenes, date "the going forth of the commandment to restore and to build Jerusalem" from "the twentieth year of Artaxerxes the king," basing their conclusion upon what is recorded in Nehemiah, chapter 2, and particularly upon Nehemiah's petition to the king, "that thou wouldest send me unto the city of my fathers' sepulchres, that I may *build it"* (Neh. 2:5). From this it is assumed that there had been up to that time no rebuilding of the city, and no previous *word* to rebuild it. This "Artaxerxes" is assumed, by those who require a late date for the decree of Dan. 9:25, to be Longimanus, whose 20th year would be nearly 80 years from the accession of Cyrus, during all of which time it is supposed (in order to suit this theory) that there had been given no permission to build the city, although permission to rebuild the Temple had been granted and acted upon, and although the inhabitants of Jerusalem had been commanded to return to it.

The first chapter of Nehemiah states that tidings were brought to Nehemiah by Hanani and certain men of Judah concerning the Jews which had returned out of captivity, and *concerning Jerusalem* (Neh. 1:2). Those brethren had reported that the returned captives were in great reproach, and that "the *wall* of Jerusalem also is broken down, and *the gates thereof* are burned with fire" (v. 3). This message was clearly occasioned by a fresh damage, recently done by the "adversaries" of the Jews, to the *walls* and *gates* of the *rebuilt* city. It was *news* to Nehemiah; for it caused him to weep, to mourn, to fast, and to pray (v. 4). The wording of the record makes it impossible to suppose that the damage reported by the messengers, who were just come from Judah, was that which had been perpetrated by Nebuchadnezzar *more than a hundred years previously.* Nehemiah had not beforetime been sad in the king's presence, but now his grief could not be controlled or concealed (2:1-2), which makes it certain that it was a new and unexpected calamity that had befallen the beloved city. This, moreover, agrees perfectly with Nehemiah's petition that he might return and "build" the city; for that word is of broad signification, one of its common meanings being to *repair* (see *Strong's Concordance*). Such is its meaning here, as is evident from the detailed account of the work in chapter 3, where the only *building* spoken of is the *repairing* of the *walls* and gates, the very parts reported by Hanani as having been injured. The word "repaired" is used over thirty times in that chapter, being used interchangeable with "builded." Moreover, the existence of *houses* is referred to incidentally in the chapter (vv. 10, 16, 20 &c.). That the work was comparatively a small one is evident from the fact that it was completed within the short space of 52 days (6:15).

But we have also to explain the statement of chapter 7:4, "Now the city was large and great [*broad in spaces,* see marg.] and the houses not builded." This, however, is easily explained. To begin with, the passage describes a state of things which existed *after Nehemiah's work was completed,* and hence it cannot, in any view of the matter, be taken to mean that the city had not been rebuilt. The meaning is evidently that there were yet wide unoccupied spaces wherein the houses had not been erected.

We would at this point bring to mind again the fact that the Seventy Weeks were to start, not from the *building* of the city (much less from its completion) but "from the *going forth of the word* to restore and to build it." In Ezra 1:1-4 we have the record of a word *going forth,* which word perfectly fulfilled the prophecies both of Isaiah and Jeremiah, which also perfectly answered the prayer of Daniel, and which perfectly corresponds with the words of Gabriel. Moreover, the Scripture gives great prominence to this decree of Cyrus, and the date thereof is stated in two passages (2 Chr. 36:22, and Ezra 1:1).

On the other hand, in Neh. 2, there is nothing that answers at all to the words of the angel, no commandment or decree going forth; but merely *letters* given to Nehemiah granting him safe conduct as far as Jerusalem (v. 7); and to the keeper of the king's forest, that he give timber for the *gates,* and for the *wall* of the city, and for the house which Nehemiah was to enter into.

Finally, the epoch-making decree of Cyrus is related to the entire scheme of Bible chronology; for it was seventy years from the beginning of the captivity; whereas the 20th year of Artaxerxes, mentioned in Neh. 2, is an uncertainty. The word "Artaxerxes" is a title (meaning *chief-ruler)* given to all the Persian kings. Some think the ruler referred to in Nehemiah is Darius (Hystaspes), and the same as the Ahasuerus of Esther. Others think he was Longimanus, who followed Xerxes and Artabanus. In the present state of knowledge this question cannot be settled. But, as to Cyrus, there is no uncertainty at all.

There are other points of interest connected with the decree of Cyrus, but for a discussion of these we must refer our readers to the book mentioned above, *The Seventy Weeks and the Great Tribulation.*

## III. "Unto the Messiah"

The words "unto the Messiah the Prince" define the goal toward which the long chronological line of the Bible had been steadily extending itself. In the days of Daniel the voice of prophecy was about to cease, and the inspired history of God's ancient people was about to come to an end. But, before the sacred record closed, the last stage of the chronology of the Old Testament was made known to "Daniel the Prophet" and by him was recorded in "the Scriptures of Truth." From the going forth of the decree of Cyrus, unto the greater Deliverer, of whom Cyrus was a remarkable type, was to be a stretch of sixty-nine "sevens" of years.

The words "unto the Messiah" tell us with all requisite clearness and certainty to just what point in the life-time of Jesus Christ the measure of 69 sevens (483 years) reaches. The word Messiah (equivalent to the Greek *Christos)* means "the Anointed." We ask, therefore, where, in the earth-life of our Lord, was He *anointed* and presented to Israel? The answer is clearly given in the Gospels and Acts. It was at *His baptism in Jordan;* for then it was that the Holy Spirit descended upon Him in bodily shape as a dove; and then it was that John the Baptist bore witness to Him as the Son of God, and the Lamb of God. As the apostle Peter declared: "God *anointed* Jesus of Nazareth with the Holy Ghost and with power" (Acts 10:38); and from that time He gave Himself to His public Messianic ministry as a "minister of the circumcision."

To this important matter we have also the Lord's own testimony. For, after His return in the power of the Spirit to Galilee, where, according to Isa. 9:1-2, the "Great Light" was to arise (see also Mat. 3:12-16), He went on the Sabbath day into the synagogue in Nazareth, and read from the prophet Isaiah these memorable words: *"The Spirit of the Lord* is upon me, because he hath *anointed me* to preach the Gospel to the poor"; and then, having sat down, and the eyes of all being fastened intently upon Him, he said, *"This day is this Scripture fulfilled in your ears"* (Luke 4:16-21). Thus the Lord declared Himself to be *at that time* the "Anointed" One, that is, *the Messiah.*

John the Baptist was sent to *"bear witness"* of Christ, and "that he should be *made manifest to Israel"* (John 1:6-7, 31). This special ministry of John was discharged by him at the time of Christ's baptism. When, therefore, the Lord Jesus had been "anointed" with the Holy Spirit, and had been "made manifest to Israel" by the witness of John, *then* the words of the prophecy "unto the Anointed One "were *completely* fulfilled. From that great and wonderful event, down to the day of His death, He was constantly before the people of Israel in His Messianic character, and was devoting Himself continuously to the fulfilling of His Messianic service, in going about doing good, manifesting the Father's Name, doing the Father's works, speaking the Father's words, healing the sick, giving sight to the blind, cleansing the lepers, raising the dead, and preaching the glad-tidings of the Kingdom of God.

Indeed, even before He announced Himself in the synagogue in Nazareth as God's "Anointed One," He had plainly said to the woman of Samaria (when she spoke of *"Messiah,* who is called *Christ")* *"I that speak unto thee am he"* (John 4:25-26). Moreover, to the Samaritans who came out to see Him upon hearing the woman's report and her question, "Is not this *the Messiah?",* He so fully revealed Himself that they were constrained to confess Him, saying, "We have heard him ourselves, and know that this is indeed *the Christ* [the *Anointed One*], the Saviour of the world" (v. 42).

Again, the purpose, as well as the effect, of the ministry of John the Baptist's public testimony to Christ is clearly revealed by the words of those who, upon hearing that testimony, followed Him. We read that "One of the two who heard John speak and followed him [Jesus] was Andrew, Simon Peter's brother. He first findeth his own brother and saith unto him, We have found *the Messias,* which is, being interpreted, *the Christ"* (John 1:40-41).

In these Scriptures the Holy Spirit has caused the important fact that Jesus was *the Anointed One* to be stated both in Hebrew and in Greek, so that the significance of it should not be lost. That "this Jesus is *the Christ"* is the great point of apostolic testimony (Acts 17:3); and it is the substance of "our faith," for "Whosoever believeth that *Jesus* is *the Christ* is born of God" (1 John 5:1, 4-5). It is also the Rock-foundation upon which He builds His church (Mat. 16:18; 1 Cor. 3:11).

Thus the Spirit of God has been pleased to give us proof upon proof that, from our Lord's baptism and manifestation to Israel, He was, in the fullest sense, *the Messiah* or the Anointed of God. Manifestly there was no *previous* event in the earthly lifetime of our Lord which could be taken as meeting in any way the words of Gabriel. And it is equally clear that no *subsequent* event could be taken as the fulfillment of those words. For there was, and could be, no subsequent occasion when the Lord was any more the "Anointed One" than when the Spirit descended upon Him at His baptism. Thus the Scriptures absolutely shut us up to the Lord's baptism, as the occasion when He was *Anointed,* and presented to Israel in His Messianic office. His baptism then marked the termination of the 69 weeks of Dan. 9:25, and the beginning of the last of the seventy weeks.

Furthermore, in addition to the foregoing evidences, we have the culminating proof found in the fact that this epoch (His Baptism), and *this alone,* is *formally dated in the Scriptures* and that His age at the time is stated. For in Luke 3:1-3 the era of the preaching and baptism of John is given with extraordinary particularity, which certifies to us that that era has a place of special importance in connection with the chronology of Scripture as a whole. It is an impressive fact that both the decree of Cyrus, and the baptism of John – that is to say, both the beginning and the ending of the sixty-nine weeks – are set forth with the greatest particularity, and that they are given with reference to the reigns of *Gentile rulers.* One is given as occurring "in the first year of Cyrus, king of Persia," and the other "in the fifteenth year of the reign of Tiberius Caesar." This is a clear indication that the things which were to be consummated within the "determined" period of seventy weeks were matters which concerned, not the Jews only, but all mankind, having to do with the salvation of Gentiles as well as Jews. God's dealings theretofore had been matters of *Jewish* history; but now, beginning with the voice of one crying in the wilderness, "Prepare ye the way of the Lord," a new era was beginning, one in which God's dealings were to be matters of *world*-history. It is appropriate, therefore, that we should have at this precise point a change from terms of Jewish to terms of Gentile chronology.

# CHAPTER FIFTEEN

## The One Week and the Fulness of the Time

We have seen that 69 of the 70 prophetic weeks were completed at the baptism of our Lord and His manifestation to Israel through the testimony of John the Baptist. This leaves but "one week" (Dan. 9:27) of the prophetic period. That week is, in the prophecy, set apart from the other 69, and we may clearly see the reason for this in the fact that in that "week" occurred the most stupendous events of all time and of all creation. For that is the period wherein God was manifested in the flesh, ministering to His sinful creatures, wherein He made atonement for the sins of His people, and wherein the Holy Spirit came down from heaven and the Kingdom of heaven was opened to all believers.

We do not discuss in these pages the view, held and taught by some, that the 70th week of the prophecy of Dan. 9 is disconnected from the other 69, and is yet in the future, and that Dan. 9:27 has to do, not with Christ, but with Antichrist; for we have discussed that view quite fully in the book already mentioned, *The Seventy Weeks and the Great Tribulation*. It will suffice for the purposes of this book to point out that the expression "seventy weeks," as a measure of time, can only mean *continuous,* or *consecutive,* weeks. Moreover, if the measure be broken off at the end of the 69th week, the great events with which the prophecy is concerned – the "cutting off" of the Messiah (thus finishing the transgression, making an end of sin, making reconciliation for iniquity, etc.) – would be left *outside the seventy weeks altogether.* It is enough, thereforc, for our present purposes, to say that the view referred to seems to us to be quite destitute of support in the Scriptures, and contrary to the terms of the prophecy itself. It should, however, be pointed out that the words "for one week" in Dan. 9:27 A. V. do not give the sense of the original, there being no "for" in the text, nor anything to imply it. The sense of the passage, as given in the Septuagint version, which our Lord quoted in Mat. 24:15, is that the "one week" (the last of the 70, of which 69 had been previously accounted for) would witness the confirming of the new covenant with many (see Mat. 26:28, noting the words "covenant" and "many"), whereby the sacrifices and oblation of the old covenant were caused to cease (see Heb. 10:9), and the things predicted in verse 24 were fulfilled.

It was "in the midst of the week," as stated in Dan. 9:27, that Christ was crucified; for His ministry lasted between three and four years, as appears by the Gospel of John, and as agreed by chronologers generally. The last verse is certainly appropriate, indeed is necessary, to complete the prophecy concerning Christ, whereas, to assign that verse to Antichrist is to intrude into the prophecy an element utterly foreign to it, and which destroys its unity. It also destroys the effect of the marvelous fulfillment, through the Cross and Resurrection of the Lord Jesus, of this wonderful prophecy.

## "The Time" Fulfilled

We believe the first proclamation of Christ, recorded most fully in Mark 1:14-15, had reference to this wonderful "time," the 70th week of the prophecy. Indeed, we do not see how there can be any reasonable question about it; for it was just at the beginning of that 70th week that He "came into Galilee, preaching the gospel of the kingdom of God, and saying, *The time is fulfilled,* and the kingdom of God is at hand; repent ye and believe the gospel." The 70th week had now come, for the 69th had brought us only "unto the Messiah." That week is the only "time" whose measure had been given in the unfulfilled prophetic Scriptures. It was *the Time* of all times, the time of Immanuel, wherein the incarnate Son of God came to preach, to heal, to bless, to die for the sins of His creatures, to rise again, and to enter upon His high-priestly ministry in heaven, the time wherein the Holy Spirit came down to abide with men, and the Kingdom of heaven began with the preaching of the gospel of God.

We have seen that the birth of Christ was in the year An. Hom. 4041, or B.C. 5. Hence the Lord's 30th year, corresponding to the 15th of Tiberius Caesar, would be A.D. 26, and His death, resurrection and ascension, and the coming of the Holy Spirit would be A.D. 30. Christ prayed on the cross for His murderers, "Father forgive them," and the answer is seen in the fact that God withheld the judgment – the destruction of Jerusalem, foretold by Daniel and by the Lord (Mat. 24; Luke 21) – for *just forty years* – for Jerusalem was destroyed by the armies of Titus, "the people of the prince that shall come," in A.D. 70 – during which period the gospel of God's grace was diligently preached "to the Jew first," and tens of thousands were saved.

Thus the history of the children of Israel began and ended with a probationary period of 40 years. The first period of 40 years' probation began with the sacrifice of the paschal lamb in Egypt; the second began with the anti-type, the Sacrifice of Jesus Christ, the true Paschal Lamb. At the close of the first of those periods God brought the people of Israel unto the land which He had promised to their fathers. At the close of the second He drove them out of that land, and scattered them among all the nations of the world.

## The Wonder of Bible Chronology

In conclusion we would again direct attention to the remarkable fact, which to the author is the outstanding Wonder of Bible Chronology, that there is one, and only one, continuous line of dated events in the Bible; that it extends from the creation of Adam to the resurrection of Christ; and that, as we follow that line through successive Books and successive eras, it brings us into contact with all the leading personages, the leading events, and the leading doctrines of Holy Scripture. Clearly then, the Chronology of the Bible must be reckoned among its greatest wonders.

www.ingramcontent.com/pod-product-compliance
Lightning Source LLC
Chambersburg PA
CBHW072017040426
42447CB00009B/1657
*9780692361764*